SOUTHWEST ROCK CLIMBING
SoCal Select

SOUTHWEST ROCK CLIMBING

SoCal Select

Randy Vogel

Chockstone Press
Evergreen, Colorado

SOUTHWEST ROCK CLIMBING: **SoCal Select**

ISBN 0-93461-62-5

Published and distributed by:
Chockstone Press, Inc.
Post Office Box 3505
Evergreen, Colorado 80439

Cover photos by Kevin Powell:
    Jonny Woodward on *Pope on a Rope* 5.12d, Joshua Tree
    Mike Waugh on *Boulder One*, Stoney Point

Editing and layout by Debra Alford
Maps by Gloria Serena, Tracy Salcedo, and Debra Alford
Hand-drawn maps and topos by Randy Vogel

This book's text is set in 10-point Optimum.

WARNING: CLIMBING IS A SPORT WHERE YOU MAY BE SERIOUSLY INJURED OR DIE.

READ THIS BEFORE YOU USE THIS BOOK.

This guidebook is a compilation of unverified information gathered from many different climbers. The author cannot assure the accuracy of any of the information in this book, including the topos and route descriptions, the difficulty ratings, and the protection ratings. These may be incorrect or misleading and it is impossible for any one author to climb all the routes to confirm the information about each route. Also, ratings of climbing difficulty and danger are always subjective and depend on the physical characteristics (for example, height), experience, technical ability, confidence and physical fitness of the climber who supplied the rating. Additionally, climbers who achieve first ascents sometimes underrate the difficulty or danger of the climbing route out of fear of being ridiculed if a climb is later down-rated by subsequent ascents. Therefore, be warned that you must exercise your own judgment on where a climbing route goes, its difficulty and your ability to safely protect yourself from the risks of rock climbing. Examples of some of these risks are: falling due to technical difficulty or due to natural hazards such as holds breaking, falling rock, climbing equipment dropped by other climbers, hazards of weather and lightning, your own equipment failure, and failure or absence of fixed protection.

You should not depend on any information gleaned from this book for your personal safety; your safety depends on your own good judgment, based on experience and a realistic assessment of your climbing ability. If you have any doubt as to your ability to safely climb a route described in this book, do not attempt it.

The following are some ways to make your use of this book safer:

1. **CONSULTATION:** You should consult with other climbers about the difficulty and danger of a particular climb prior to attempting it. Most local climbers are glad to give advice on routes in their area and we suggest that you contact locals to confirm ratings and safety of particular routes and to obtain first-hand information about a route chosen from this book.

2. **INSTRUCTION:** Most climbing areas have local climbing instructors and guides available. We recommend that you engage an instructor or guide to learn safety techniques and to become familiar with the routes and hazards of the areas described in this book. Even after you are proficient in climbing safely, occasional use of a guide is a safe way to raise your climbing standard and learn advanced techniques.

3. **FIXED PROTECTION:** Many of the routes in this book use bolts and pitons which are permanently placed in the rock. Because of variances in the manner of placement, weathering, metal fatigue, the quality of the metal used, and many other factors, these fixed protection pieces should always be considered suspect and should always be backed up by equipment that you place yourself. Never depend for your safety on a single piece of fixed protection because you never can tell whether it will hold weight, and in some cases, fixed protection may have been removed or is now absent.

Be aware of the following specific potential hazards which could arise in using this book:

1. **MISDESCRIPTIONS OF ROUTES:** If you climb a route and you have a doubt as to where the route may go, you should not go on unless you are sure that you can go that way safely. Route descriptions and topos in this book may be inaccurate or misleading.

2. **INCORRECT DIFFICULTY RATING:** A route may, in fact, be more difficult than the rating indicates. Do not be lulled into a false sense of security by the difficulty rating.

3. **INCORRECT PROTECTION RATING:** If you climb a route and you are unable to arrange adequate protection from the risk of falling through the use of fixed pitons or bolts and by placing your own protection devices, do not assume that there is adequate protection available higher just because the route protection rating indicates the route is not an "X" or an "R" rating. Every route is potentially an "X" (a fall may be deadly), due to the inherent hazards of climbing – including, for example, failure or absence of fixed protection, your own equipment's failure, or improper use of climbing equipment.

THERE ARE NO WARRANTIES, WHETHER EXPRESS OR IMPLIED, THAT THIS GUIDEBOOK IS ACCURATE OR THAT THE INFORMATION CONTAINED IN IT IS RELIABLE. THERE ARE NO WARRANTIES OF FITNESS FOR A PARTICULAR PURPOSE OR THAT THIS GUIDE IS MERCHANTABLE. YOUR USE OF THIS BOOK INDICATES YOUR ASSUMPTION OF THE RISK THAT IT MAY CONTAIN ERRORS AND IS AN ACKNOWLEDGEMENT OF YOUR OWN SOLE RESPONSIBILITY FOR YOUR CLIMBING SAFETY.

Preface

Road trips are a climber's dream; most of us love to "hit the road" and explore new climbing areas. Nothing revitalizes your psyche for climbing like visiting a new area. Sometimes, a business trip or otherwise interminable family vacation, reunion, etc., puts you momentarily in the vicinity of climbable rock. Yet limited time (and often money) mean that investing in a trunkload of guidebooks doesn't always make sense.

In such situations, you are usually at the mercy of hand-drawn maps and scribbled bits of paper listing "recommended" routes. Frequently you miss out on a great spot because you didn't hear about it or couldn't find it. These guidebooks were written for you.

The inspiration for this series of guides was pure laziness. I have often befriended a traveling European, or a pale winter refugee of colder climes. First, I innocently recommend a visit to some area while on their sojourn, then I get hooked into drawing a map and some topos and suggesting routes to climb. Now, I can merely suggest that they "buy the book."

Of course, like all guidebook projects, my indolence has again tricked me; guidebooks never fly together on their own. But once committed, there is no safe way to retreat. So I do the next best thing – I enlist the help of others. For this first volume, many people provided valuable help. In particular I would like to thank Sarah Tringali, for putting up with visiting all these places ("You don't mind if we check out one more route?"); Bill Freeman, Kevin Powell and Troy Mayr for providing photos to liven up the book; Bob Gaines for the nice shots of Tahquitz & Suicide Rocks; and Louie Anderson for beta on the Pine Creek area.

Please respect the unique environments you will encounter, and leave them in better shape than when you got there. Finally, I hope that you have as much fun using this guide as I had investigating the routes listed.

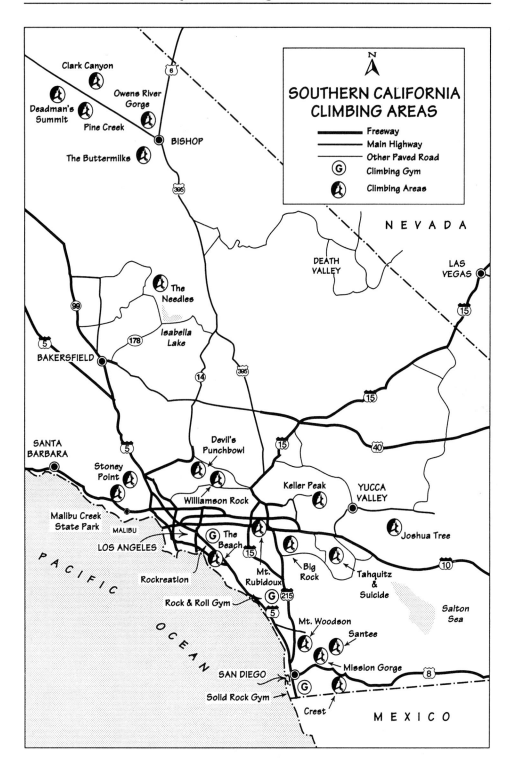

SOUTHWEST ROCK CLIMBING
SoCal Select

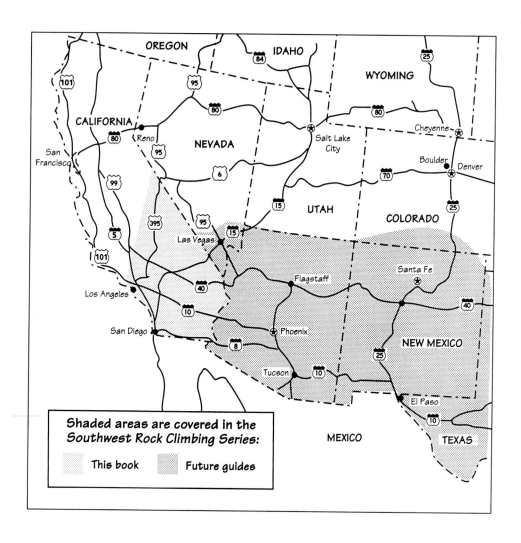

Shaded areas are covered in the
Southwest Rock Climbing Series:

This book   Future guides

Introduction

The American southwest is blessed with a multitude of good climbs and climbing areas. As many of these areas have become more developed, they have sprouted their own comprehensive guidebooks. At some areas, information is spread by word of mouth, in magazine articles, or compiled on sheets of paper in local climbing stores. However, the infrequent or traveling climber may not have the time (or money) to gather all this information or purchase every guidebook.

This is the first in a series of guides that will cover selected climbs (and areas) in the American southwest. Each volume will provide concise information on many climbing and bouldering areas at an affordable price. Every attempt has been made to make the information concise and easy to use. Detailed road and overview maps are provided to help you find the best way to get to any area.

If you plan a long visit to any particular spot, or will be climbing there with some regularity, you may want to invest in a comprehensive guidebook for that area (local guidebooks are usually referenced for each area). Also, the selection of routes and information included in this guidebook reflect both the biases of the author and constraints on space. Even so, the climbs selected for this book generally reflect the better routes of an area.

Southern California

This first volume covers southern California, beginning with the climbing areas around Mammoth Lakes/Owens River Gorge in the north, to The Needles in the southern Sierra Nevada, to Joshua Tree in the high desert, to the wide variety of areas surrounding Los Angeles, to Mount Woodson and other areas near San Diego. With the exception of The Needles, climbs in the Sierra Nevada are not covered.

How this Guide Works

For each climbing or bouldering area, information is provided on the best season, the type of equipment needed, and a listing of any comprehensive guidebooks that might be available. A brief summary of the type of climbing available is also given. Maps and/or directions are provided to help you get to each area. The overview map next to the table of contents notes the relative location of each area (and can be used as a driving aid), but the use of a good road map or road atlas is recommended.

At the top of each page are the name of the climbing area and (where appropriate) the specific section of the area where the routes described are located.

For major climbing and bouldering areas, selected routes/problems are described. Detailed topographic route descriptions, in conjunction with detailed maps, are used to describe climbs. (See the explanation of topo symbols and a map legend on page 2.) In some cases, written descriptions will supplement this information. For other areas, specific route information and/or topos may be omitted. In most cases, there should be little need to consult other guidebooks.

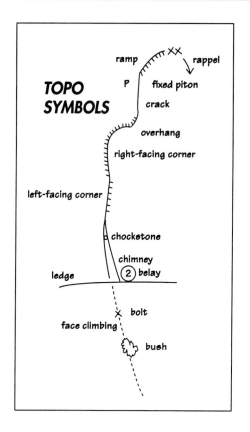

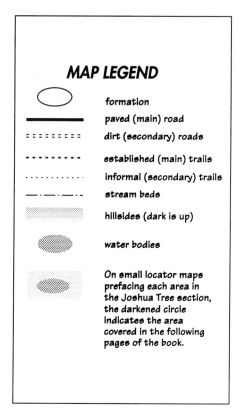

Ratings

All the climbs listed in this guide are given a difficulty rating, and where applicable, a quality and/or protection rating. The notation (TR) indicates a top-rope climb.

Difficulty Ratings

The difficulty rating system used in this guidebook is the Tahquitz Decimal System, (also known – erroneously – as the Yosemite Decimal System, or YDS). This system is used throughout the United States, and most climbers will be familiar with its idiosyncrasies.

Climbing routes are rated on an ascending scale from 5.0 (the easiest climbs requiring ropes and belays) to 5.14 (currently the most difficult climbs). Within the 5.10, 5.11, 5.12, 5.13 and 5.14 categories, the subgrades of a, b, c and d are used to denote finer distinctions in difficulty.

Climbers may find the ratings at a particular area are harder or easier than other areas. Although the ratings given to routes in this guide are generally consistent, *the ratings given to some routes may just be wrong.*

A Rating Comparison Chart is included here to assist foreign climbers in determining the relative difficulty of the climbs listed.

International Rating Systems Compared

West German	YDS	British	Australian	East German	French
	5.0				
	5.1				
	5.2				
	5.3				
	5.4				
	5.5				
	5.6				
5+	5.7	4b — VS		VIIa	5a
6-	5.8	4c	15	VIIb	5b
6	5.9	HVS	16 / 17	VIIb	5c
6+	5.10a	5a — E1	18	VIIc	6a
7-	5.10b	5b	19	VIIIa	6a+
7	5.10c	E2	20	VIIIb	6b
7+	5.10d		21	VIIIc	6b+
8-	5.11a	5c — E3	22	IXa	6c
8	5.11b		22	IXb	6c+
8	5.11c	6a	23	IXc	6c+
8+	5.11d	E4	24	IXc	7a
9-	5.12a		25	Xa	7a+
9	5.12b	6b — E5	26	Xb	7b
9	5.12c		27	Xb	7b+
9+	5.12d		28	Xc	7c
10-	5.13a	6c — E6	28		7c+
10	5.13b	7a	29		8a
10	5.13c		30		8a+
10+	5.13d	E7	31		8b
11-	5.14a		32		8b+

Quality Ratings

A "star" or "quality" rating is used in this guide. This system is designed to key climbers to better climbs.

Climbs are given no stars if they are considered just average or less in quality, and one through three stars (on an ascending scale) if they are thought to be better routes. Three-star routes are acknowledged classics. This system is highly subjective. Consequently, use it as an indication only, and remember that many unstarred routes may in fact be worthy of your attention (and vice versa).

Protection Ratings

In this guidebook, "R" and "X" protection ratings are given. However, what constitutes good protection for one climber may be poor protection to another. This is especially true when climbing "traditional" routes (placing your own pro). If your protection skills are rusty or undeveloped, you may find some routes very difficult to adequately protect. Little consensus exists for protection ratings, so do not rely on the absence of a protection rating to indicate good protection. Use common sense.

R Rating: Poorly protected at the hard spots. A very long or serious fall possible. (Technically, a long or even deadly fall could occur on almost any route).

X Rating: Extremely poorly protected at the hard spots. A severe fall, (e.g. hitting a deck) is possible. Could result in severe injury or death.

The R and X ratings in this guide are intended to be used as a guideline only. Only you can be the judge of whether a route is adequately enough protected for you. Many easier routes that deserve a protection rating may not have them. **Never assume a route without a protection rating is safe.** You, alone, are responsible for your own safe climbing.

Minimize Your Impact

Rock climbers can constitute a significant percentage of visitors to a particular climbing area. For this reason climbers must take particular care to ensure that their visit has as minimal an environmental impact as possible. Although climbers tend, as a group, to be some of the most environmentally conscientious users, there is a growing, and often critical, look being taken at climbing activities throughout the United States.

About Trash, Poot Slings and Other Forms of Pollution

One of the most tangible forms of environmental impact which climbers have is the refuse they leave behind. This trash takes many forms, but the most common and serious forms of trash pollution are discarded (used) tape, improperly disposed-of human waste (including toilet paper), and "poot" slings.

While there is absolutely no excuse for ever leaving used tape behind (it will easily fit into your pack or pocket), convenient toilet facilities are not available in many climbing areas in this book. Use toilets where available, and use other facilities before you hike into places where there are no toilets. Climbers must use common sense and care where toilets are not available.

A few rules should be observed. Do not ever leave human waste anywhere near waterways or dry stream beds. In desert areas, human waste decomposes most quickly when not buried. In more moist climates, dig a small hole (six inches or so), and bury or cover any feces. In all cases, soiled paper should be carried out in a small resealable plastic bag; this is the only way to ensure that the environment does not have to struggle for years to decompose it on its own.

"Poot" slings (runners left on fixed protection or anchors) are an unsightly and unnecessary form of pollution. Rock-colored webbing is now available at almost every climbing shop. Every climber should carry some of this webbing so that if it is necessary to leave webbing behind, it will not clash with the rock color. Of course, whenever a climber encounters any webbing left by an earlier climber, it makes sense to remove it and dispose of it.

About Chipping, Gluing and Bolting

It is currently illegal throughout the National Park System to use motorized drills, chip holds or use glue to add or reinforce a hold. Please abide by these restrictions when climbing in any National Park or Monument. Chipping holds is a questionable practice in *any* climbing area, as it robs future climbers of the ability to establish yet harder and harder routes. Chipping is strongly discouraged.

Corrections

Sometimes information in this guidebook may not be entirely clear or may have inaccuracies. Please send any corrections to the author at P.O. Box 4554, Laguna Beach, CA 92652. All corrections and suggestions are welcome.

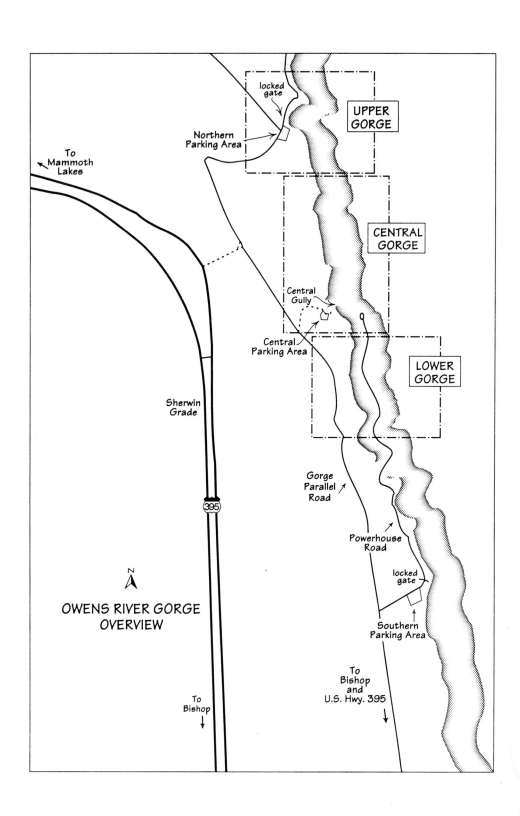

Owens River Gorge

In the Owens Valley east of the High Sierra, the Owens River has cut a deep gorge into the volcanic rocks that lie just north of the town of Bishop, California. Vertical and overhanging face climbing with good holds and pockets are the predominant types of climbing. Most routes are entirely bolt-protected, and with few exceptions, quickdraws are the only gear needed.

Bishop and Mammoth Lakes have a significant local population of climbers. However, Owens River Gorge is also popular with climbers from Los Angeles and the San Francisco Bay Areas. As word of mouth has spread, the Gorge has also become a destination for climbers from throughout the United States and Europe.

The Gorge is located on property owned by the Los Angeles Department of Water and Power (DWP). The DWP operates power-generating equipment in the Gorge and has been very gracious in allowing climbing in the Gorge. Climbers have a responsibility to ensure that they are good guests on DWP property to ensure this fabulous climbing area remains accessible. Be courteous to DWP personnel at all times.

Access Rules

- Do not block or park in front of any of the gates.
- No motorized vehicles beyond the gates.
- Do not involve DWP in any accidents or rescues. (Call 911. There is a phone at Mill Creek Station, US 395, 10 miles south of the Gorge.)
- No camping on DWP property.
- Stay away from DWP equipment and yield to DWP vehicles on the roads.
- Do not leave any human waste near the water in the Gorge, and carry out all trash (not just your own).
- To minimize impact, use the trail systems that have developed.

Season

Owens River Gorge is one of only a few climbing areas that offers year-round climbing. The best times to visit are during spring, early summer, late summer and fall. While the heat of summer and cold of winter can be quite extreme, following the sun or shade can extend the season considerably.

Equipment

The Gorge is primarily a sport climbing area; most routes are bolted with fixed anchors. A few routes may require supplemental gear, and it is a good idea to bring a few small to medium camming devices. A few routes require two ropes to lower off; most require a 165-foot (50-meter) rope which should be considered a minimum.

Guidebooks

Owens River Gorge Climbs by Marty Lewis is an excellent and comprehensive "topo" format guide. It is regularly updated and supplemented. If you plan an extended stay or regular visits, it is recommended. It can be purchased at most climbing stores.

Local Climbing Shops

Wilson's Eastside Sports, 206 N. Main Street (US 395), Bishop, CA 93514. (619) 873-7520. An excellent climbing shop, also famous for fine resoling.

Pat's Backcountry Shop, located in the Sherwin Professional Plaza on Old Mammoth Road (.25 mile south of Meridian Blvd.), Mammoth Lakes, CA. (619) 934-2008.

How to get to the Gorge

The Gorge is located about 14 miles north of Bishop, California and 23 miles south of Mammoth Lakes, California, in the Owens Valley, east of the High Sierra.

From the South

From southern California, head north on either US 14 or take I-15 to US 395 and head north to the town of Bishop. See the overview map near the table of contents, page viii. From the southwest, take the best route to Bishop.

From Bishop

Take US 395 north from the town of Bishop for about 14 miles. Turn east (right) on Gorge Road to where it ends at Gorge Parallel Road. Head north (left) on Gorge Parallel Road. The Southern Parking Area is 3 miles up the road (a paved turn-off to the right). The Central Parking Area turnoff is located at about 4.5 miles (dirt). The Northern Parking Area is located at the 6-mile mark.

From the North

From northern California, head east to US 395, then south toward Mammoth Lakes. In the summer months, Owens River Gorge is a short drive from Tuolumne Meadows. During the winter months, most passes over the Sierra Nevada (except I-80) are closed, making driving to the Gorge a bit longer affair. See overview map, page viii.

From Mammoth Lakes

You can drive south from Mammoth Lakes Junction at US 395 to the Gorge Road (about 27 miles; see directions "From the South" above), or a more direct route is to drive south about 23 miles, then turn left at a not-too-obvious Caltrans access road, and then head back north on US 395. After about 0.2 mile, turn east (right) at a dirt road located off a paved turn-out. (If you go past the "scenic point" sign, you went too far.) Take the dirt road a short distance to where it meets up with Gorge Parallel Road. The Northern Parking Area is about 1 mile north, the Central Parking Area 0.5 mile south, and the Southern Parking Area 2 miles to the south.

Camping

There is no camping allowed in the Gorge, the parking areas, or on DWP property. Many excellent campgrounds are located near the Gorge. Climbers will find everything from free primitive camping to campgrounds featuring hot showers.

Free Camping

Horton Creek Campground

Open May to October. No water, pit toilets, picnic tables. From the Gorge, head south on US 395, turn right (west) at the Pine Creek exit, turn left on Round Valley Road, then go 2 miles, turning right at the sign for the campground. From Bishop, head north to the Sawmill Road exit, turn left (west), then make a fairly quick right onto Round Valley Road, which is followed until a left turn leads to the campground.

Lower Rock Creek Campground

Open April through September. No water, pit toilets, picnic tables. Head north on US 395 to Lower Rock Creek exit, turn left (west), and go 1 mile to the campground.

Other Campgrounds

There are several other campgrounds in the area that charge from $5 to $10 per night. These include: Pleasant Valley and Millpond (south of the Gorge), and Tuff Campground (north of the Gorge). All have water and Mill Pond Campground ($10 per night) has hot showers!

Food, etc.

The town of Bishop has several supermarkets. Schatts Bakery is the best place for fresh baked goods. Mammoth Lakes to the north has many good restaurants for the more discriminating climber.

Approaches to the Routes

Because the Gorge is quite long, several different approaches have developed. Depending on where you plan to climb, if you have a bicycle, or if small children are with you, some approaches may be better than others.

Generally, if you plan to climb in the Lower Gorge, the Southern Parking Area is best. The Central Parking Area is best for getting to the Central and Abandoned Gorge, and the Northern Parking Area is the fastest way to get to the Upper Gorge. However, the Southern Parking Area has a paved road leading down into the Gorge, and if you have a bicycle, this is the way to get to both the Central and Lower Gorge Areas. The Central Parking Area approach is down a steep scree chute, and may not be suitable for the timid or for small children.

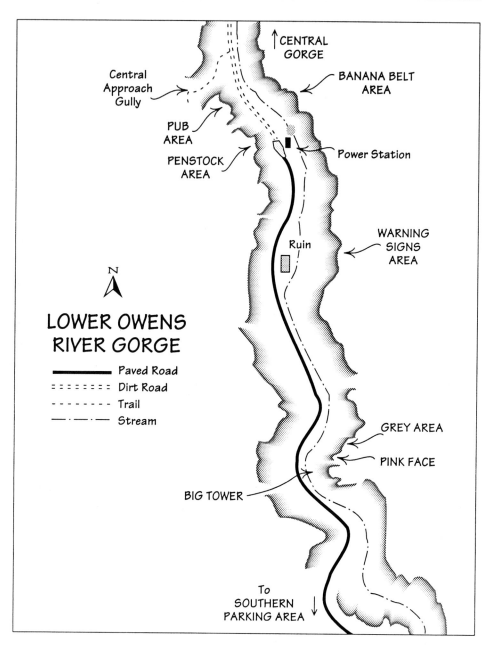

CENTRAL
GORGE

Central
Approach
Gully

BANANA BELT
AREA

PUB
AREA

PENSTOCK
AREA

Power Station

Ruin

WARNING
SIGNS
AREA

N

**LOWER OWENS
RIVER GORGE**

——————— Paved Road
= = = = = = = Dirt Road
- - - - - - - Trail
—·—·—·— Stream

GREY AREA

PINK FACE

BIG TOWER

To
SOUTHERN
PARKING AREA

Lower Gorge

The Lower Gorge is approached via the Southern Parking Area. Walk or ride your bicycle down the paved DWP road until the bottom of the Gorge is reached (approximately 0.8 mile).

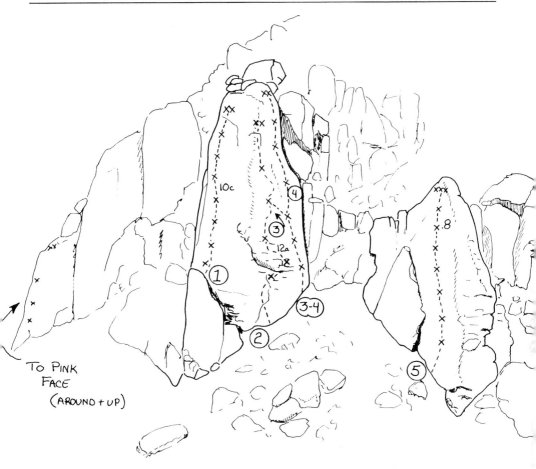

Big Tower

After reaching the bottom of the Gorge, Big Tower is the first formation encountered on the right side of the road. Morning shade, afternoon sun. See map page 10.

1 *Held Over* 5.10c ★ Pro: 7 bolts.
2 *Bust a Move* 5.12a ★ Pro: 5 bolts. (more go for it than difficult)
3 *Exit Stage Left* 5.10a Pro: 5 bolts. (easy way to set up TR on #2)
4 *Big Screen* 5.10b Pro: 6 bolts.
5 *Coming Attractions* 5.8 ★ Pro: 7 bolts.

Pink Face

This face lies around the corner and left (upstream) of Big Tower. As the name suggests, the rock has a "pinkish" patina to it. See map page 10.

6 *Wowie Zowie* 5.10a ★★ Pro: 4 bolts. Climb up the center of the Pink Face to anchors; lower or rap off.

Grey Area

This section of rock is almost always in shade. The large shade trees and streamside location make this a popular spot when it's hot. This area is located a short distance around the corner and down from Big Tower and Pink Face, by some large cottonwood trees. The routes lie on either side of a large dihedral that comes down nearly to the water's edge. See map page 10.

7 *Gunning For A Heart Attack* 5.10b ★ Pro: 4 bolts. This route is on the left side of the dihedral. A medium size nut may be helpful. (Crux is getting to the first bolt.)

8 *Grey Scale* 5.10a ★★ Pro: 4 bolts, optional to 1.5 inches. Start just right of the wide crack in the corner of the dihedral.

Kevin Powell

Bird Lew on *Embrace This*, 5.12a, Riverside Area

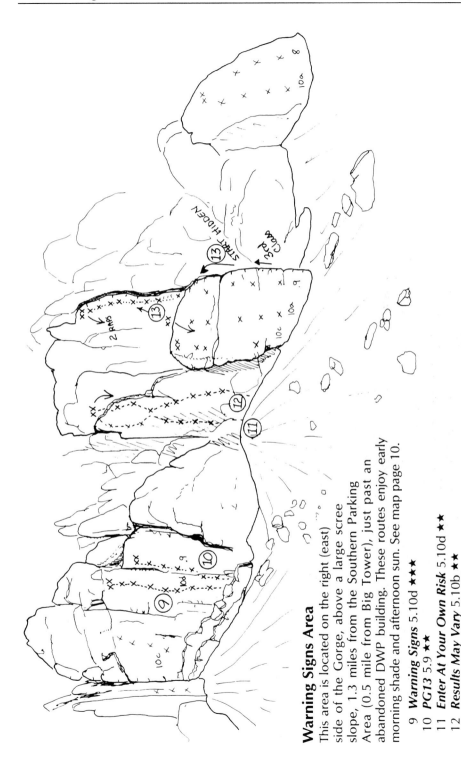

Warning Signs Area

This area is located on the right (east) side of the Gorge, above a large scree slope, 1.3 miles from the Southern Parking Area (0.5 mile from Big Tower), just past an abandoned DWP building. These routes enjoy early morning shade and afternoon sun. See map page 10.

9 *Warning Signs* 5.10d ★★★
10 *PG13* 5.9 ★★
11 *Enter At Your Own Risk* 5.10d ★★
12 *Results May Vary* 5.10b ★★
13 *Timeless* 5.10d ★★★

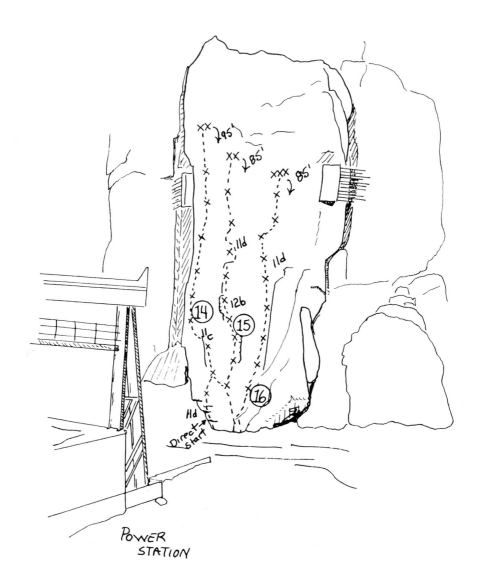

Penstock Rock

This area can be approached easily from the Central Parking Area or from the Southern Parking Area. It lies on the west side of the Gorge, where the paved road ends. A large DWP transformer station is found here. Early morning sun, shade all afternoon. See maps on pages 10 and 15.

14 **D.W.P.** 5.11c ★★★ 100 foot rap off anchors.
15 **Flashflood** 5.12a/b ★★★
16 **Pumping Groundwater** 5.11d ★★★

Central Gorge

The routes of the Central Gorge are most easily reached via the Central Parking Area. Climbers also commonly approach the Central Gorge from the Southern Parking Area (particularly if you have bicycles). See map.

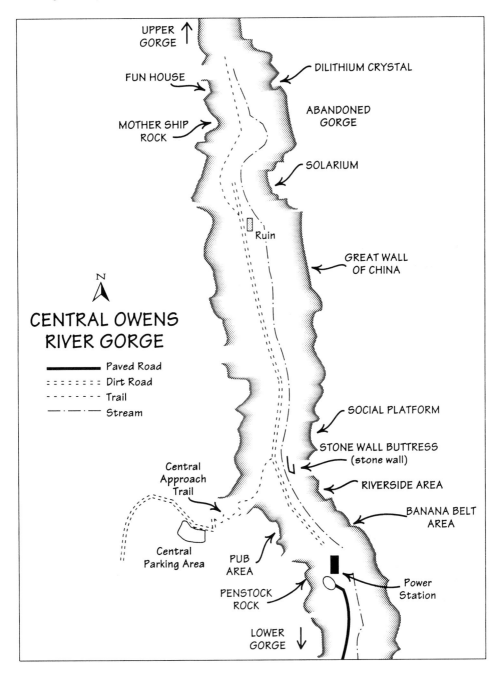

UPPER GORGE

DILITHIUM CRYSTAL

FUN HOUSE

ABANDONED GORGE

MOTHER SHIP ROCK

SOLARIUM

Ruin

GREAT WALL OF CHINA

N

CENTRAL OWENS RIVER GORGE

Paved Road
Dirt Road
Trail
Stream

SOCIAL PLATFORM

STONE WALL BUTTRESS
(stone wall)

Central Approach Trail

RIVERSIDE AREA

BANANA BELT AREA

Central Parking Area

PUB AREA

PENSTOCK ROCK

Power Station

LOWER GORGE

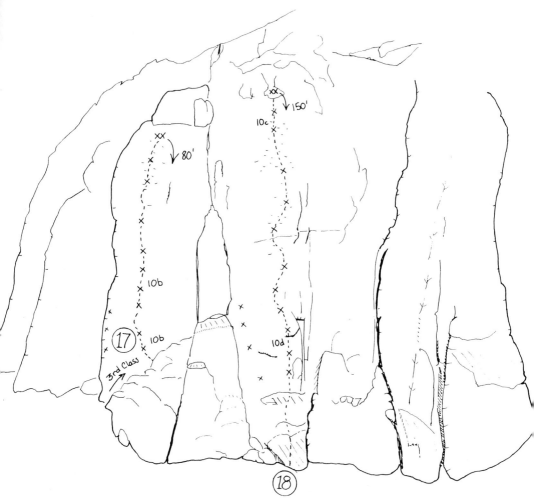

Banana Belt Area

This is really the southern part of the continuous cliffs on the east side of the Central Gorge. It faces southwest, and has sun for much of the day. See maps on pages 10 and 15.

17 *Environmental Terrorist* 5.10b ★★
18 *Love Stinks* 5.10d ★★★ 2 ropes required to descend.

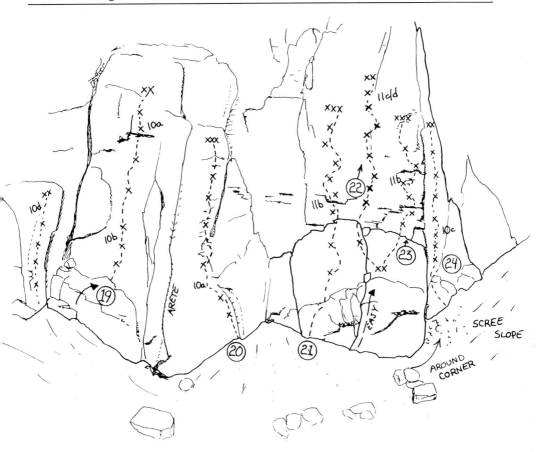

Pub Area (aka **High Tension West**)

This excellent cliff lies just south of the large scree slope below the Central Parking Area approach gully. It receives early morning sun, and is in the shade for most of the afternoon. Routes 21 to 23 are more than 85 feet long, but one rope can be used to lower. See map page 15.

19 *Gary Grey* 5.10b ★ Pro: 7 bolts.
20 *Arbitarot* 5.10a ★ Pro: 6 bolts.
21 *Hungover* 5.11b ★★★ Pro: 8 bolts.
22 *Highball* 5.11d ★ Pro: 9 bolts.
23 *Hammered* 5.11b ★★ Pro: 6 bolts.
24 *Light Within* 5.10d ★★★ Pro: 7 bolts.

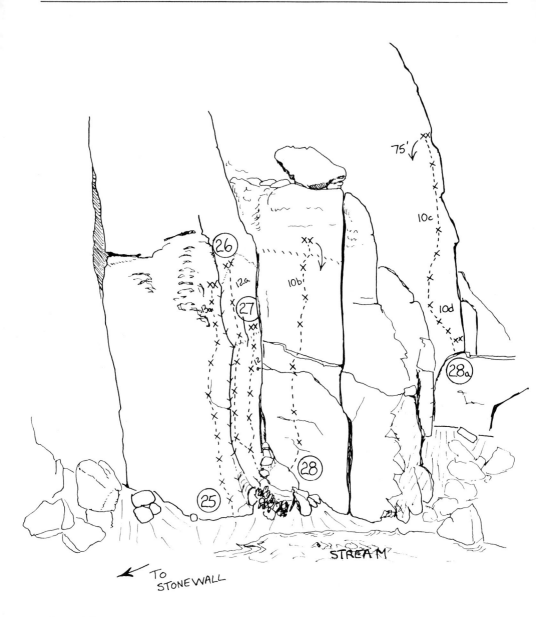

Riverside Area

This cliff is in the central part of the continuous cliffs on the east side of the Central Gorge. Early morning shade, sun most of the afternoon. See map page 15.

25   *Conquistadors Without Swords* 5.13b ★★ Pro: 10 bolts.
26   *Embrace This* 5.12a ★ Pro: 7 bolts.
27   *Hard Copy* 5.12a ★★ Pro: 6 bolts.
28   *George Bush* 5.10b ★★ Pro: 6 bolts.
28a *Brothers in Arms* 5.10d ★★ Pro: 8 bolts.

Social Platform

This cliff is in the northern part of the continuous cliffs on the east side of the Central Gorge. Early morning shade, sun most of the afternoon. Expressway and Darshan face northwest and stay in the shade a bit longer. See map page 15.

29 *Expressway* 5.11a ★★★ Pro: 8 bolts.
30 *Darshan (Rip Off)* 5.12a ★★★ Pro: 8 bolts.
31 *Ned Guy's Proud Pearl Necklace* 5.11d ★★ Pro: 6 bolts.
32 *Orange Peal* 5.10c ★★★ Pro: 6 bolts.
33 *Skeletons In The Closet* 5.11b ★★ Pro: 8 bolts.

Stonewall Buttress

This cliff is in the central part of the continuous cliffs on the east side of the Central Gorge. Early morning shade, sun most of the afternoon. See map page 15.

34 *Santana* 5.11c ★★★ Pro: 8 bolts.

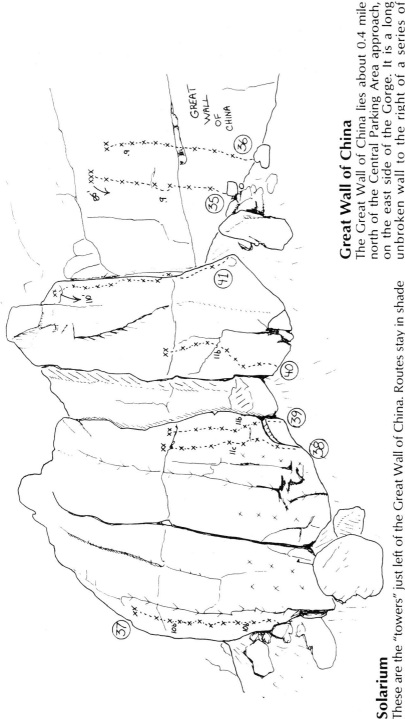

Solarium

These are the "towers" just left of the Great Wall of China. Routes stay in shade longer than the Great Wall. Morning shade, afternoon sun. See map page 15.

37 *Show Us Your Tits* 5.10b/c ★★★ Pro: 10 bolts.
38 *Venom* 5.11c ★★ Pro: 7 bolts.
39 *Cobra* 5.11b/c ★★ (roof move is height-dependent) Pro: 6 bolts.
40 *Focus* 5.11a/b ★ Pro: 7 bolts.
41 *Sendero Luminoso* 5.10b ★★★ Pro: 9 bolts, 2-rope rappel.

Great Wall of China

The Great Wall of China lies about 0.4 mile north of the Central Parking Area approach, on the east side of the Gorge. It is a long unbroken wall to the right of a series of towers. It lies almost directly across the stream from an abandoned DWP building. Early morning shade, sun all afternoon. See map page 15.

35 *Child of Light* 5.9 ★★★ Pro: 7 bolts.
36 *Heart of the Sun* 5.9 ★★★ Pro: 8 bolts.

Abandoned Gorge

The Abandoned Gorge refers to the area north of the Central Gorge and south of the Upper Gorge. It is covered in the Central Gorge map and is best approached from the Central Gorge Parking Area. This part of the Gorge narrows and the broad trail/dirt road becomes a narrow ascending path. See map page 15.

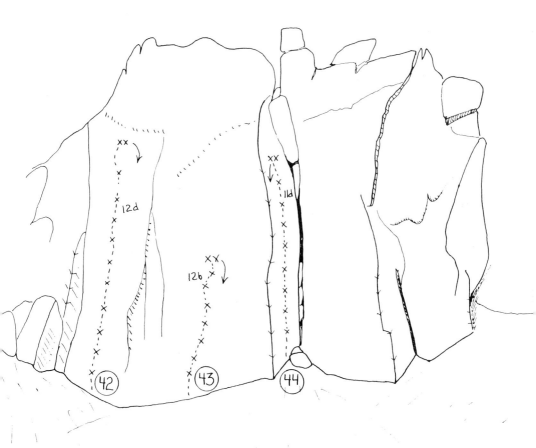

Mother Ship Rock

This formation is located on the west side of the Gorge, up scree from where the foot trail rounds the bend and begins to level off. This is some 200 yards past the abandoned DWP building. Morning sun, afternoon shade. See map page 15.

42 *Excelsior* 5.12d ★★★ Pro: 10 bolts.
43 *Piranha* 5.12b ★★★ Pro: 7 bolts.
44 *Bird of Prey* 5.11d ★★ Pro: 8 bolts.

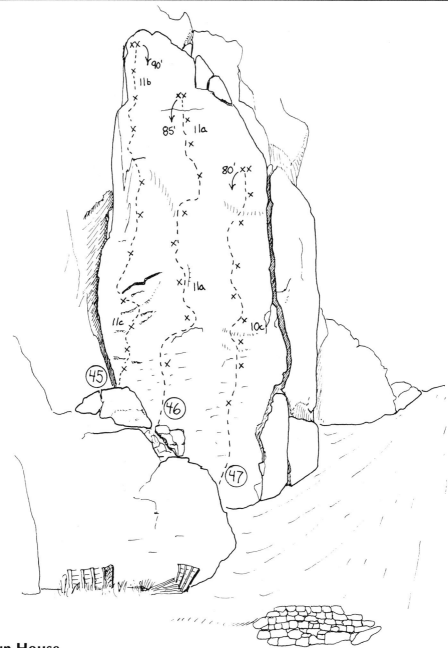

Fun House

This popular crag lies on the west side of the Gorge, just above where the foot path reaches a level platform. It is almost directly across the Gorge from the Dilithium Crystal. Morning sun, afternoon shade. See map page 15.

   45 *Thumbs Up* 5.11c ★★ Pro: 10 bolts.
   46 *Escapade* 5.11a ★★★ Pro: 8 bolts.
   47 *Melts in Your Mouth* 5.10c ★★ Pro: 8 bolts.

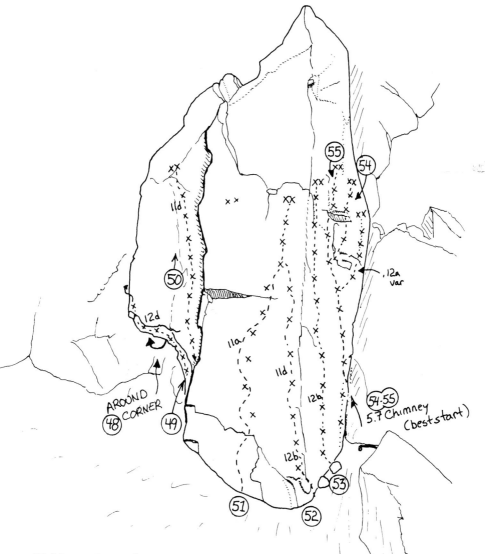

Dilithium Crystal

This large block of rock lies on the east side of the Gorge, and has many fine steep and overhanging face routes. It lies almost directly across the Gorge from the Fun House. Enterprise and Borg stay in the shade much of the day; the other climbs get early morning shade and afternoon sun. See map page 15.

  48 *Enterprise* 5.12b ★★★ Pro: 10 bolts.
  49 *Not for Sale* (aka *Borg*) 5.12d ★★ Pro: 8 bolts.
  50 *Dr. Claw* 5.11d ★★ Pro: 8 bolts.
  51 *Photon Torpedo* 5.11a ★★ Pro: 9 bolts.
  52 *Mind Meld* 5.12a/b ★★ Pro: 10 bolts.
  53 *Phasers On Stun* 5.12b ★★★ Pro: 11 bolts.
  54 *Klingon* 5.12a ★★★ Pro: 9 bolts.
  55 *Romulan Roof* 5.11d ★★ Pro: 10 bolts.

Upper Gorge

The Upper Gorge is rather isolated, and is somewhat less developed than the other sections of the Gorge. However, it has a number of excellent routes. Park at the Northern Parking Area, follow the road for about 0.25 mile, drop down a rough trail that heads down and south along the talus slope. Continue downstream, past old wooden trestles, for about 700 yards, where the gorge widens and curves right, then back left. Holy Trinity Wall is on your right (west); the obvious Gorgeous Towers, a little further down, is also on your right (west). Unlike the remainder of the Gorge, areas are described going downstream, as this is the most common way they are approached. These routes can also be approached from the Central Gorge, but this is a longer walk. See map.

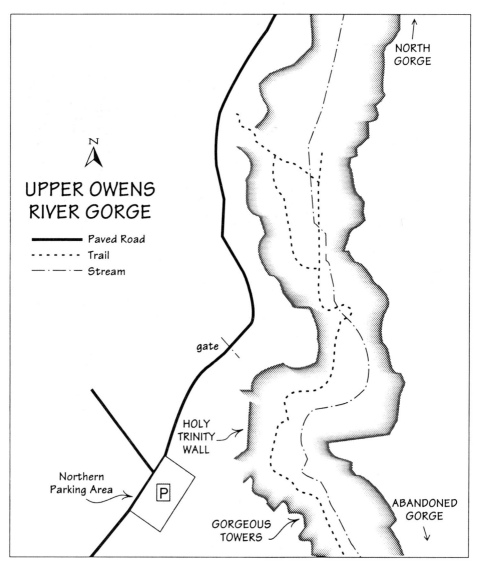

Holy Trinity Wall (No Topo)

This crag is located on the west side of the Gorge, a short distance north of Gorgeous Towers and about 500 yards south of where the approach trail reaches the bottom of the Gorge. Morning sun and afternoon shade. See map page 24.

This crag lies up away from the stream, in a somewhat recessed area. Several difficult routes will be found on this wall, to either side of the main face where the following routes lie. Easy fifth-class climbing leads to a ledge at the base of the central face. Bolts will be found on the ledge for belay anchors.

56   ***Sex*** 5.11c ★★★ Pro: 12 bolts. This is the left route; start at the left-hand anchors.

57   ***Sex Packets*** 5.12a ★★★ Pro: 8 bolts. Start at the right-hand anchors, but stay left (see below).

57a. ***Dowhatchyalike*** 5.12b ★ Pro: 6 bolts. Start at the right-hand anchors (same as Sex Packets) but head right and up after the first bolt. Ends at same point.

Kevin Powell

Suzanne Paulson on *Gorgeous*, 5.10a

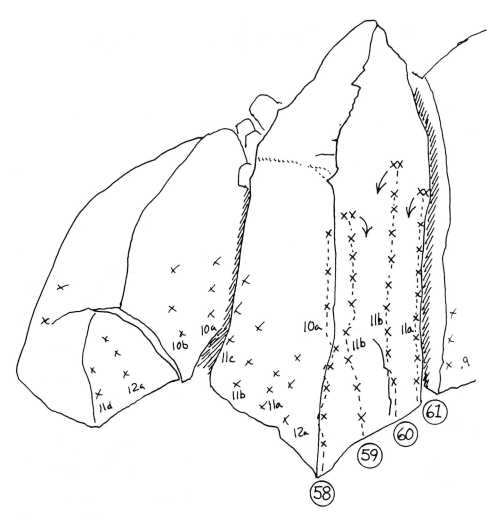

Gorgeous Towers

A popular and excellent crag, located on the west side of the Gorge, 600 yards south of where the approach trail reaches the bottom of the Gorge, about 90 yards south of Holy Trinity Wall. It is quite obvious. Partial morning sun, afternoon shade. See map page 24.

58 *Gorgeous* 5.10a ★★★ Pro: 8 bolts.
59 *C'mon Knucko* 5.11b ★★ Pro: 8 bolts.
60 *Knucko's Pride of the North* 5.11a/b ★★ Pro: 9 bolts.
61 *The-Arêtical* 5.11a ★★ Pro: 8 bolts

Pine Creek Canyon

This granite area (also known as Pratt's Crack Buttress/Scheelite) is located close to Owens River Gorge and offers cooler temperatures, making it an ideal place for a short visit during the summer. Although a number of traditional crack climbs are found here, recent development of steep, bolted sport routes have made this a popular spot with locals. The climbing is unusual and requires a multitude of techniques.

How to get to Pine Creek

Pine Creek Road is found 9 miles north of Bishop off Highway 395. From Highway. 395, turn west on Pine Creek Road; follow it for about 7.5 miles (pass through small town of Rovana) to where a paved road heads off to the right (private). Another rough dirt road heads off at a sharper right. At this point, the sharp arête of Ecstasy (5.13a) can be seen clearly on the left side of the narrow canyon above and right of the Pine Creek Road. Park here and walk (or drive) up the dirt road (high clearance/4WD required); a short walk leads to the steep walls to either side of the obvious off-width crack in the corner (Pratt's Crack, 5.9). (See map page 30.)

Season

Pine Creek is primarily a summer area, receiving virtually no sun in the winter months. In summer, most of the climbs go into the shade by 10 am.

Equipment

Although many "traditional" gear climbs are found in the immediate vicinity, most of the routes described here are sport-type routes. Quickdraws are the only gear you need bring for most climbs, although you might bring some gear if Pratt's Crack or Sheila attract your attention. A few routes require two ropes to lower off; some require a 165-foot (50-meter) rope, which should be considered a minimum.

Local Climbing Shops

Wilson's Eastside Sports, 206 N. Main Street (US 395), Bishop, CA 93514. (619) 873-7520.

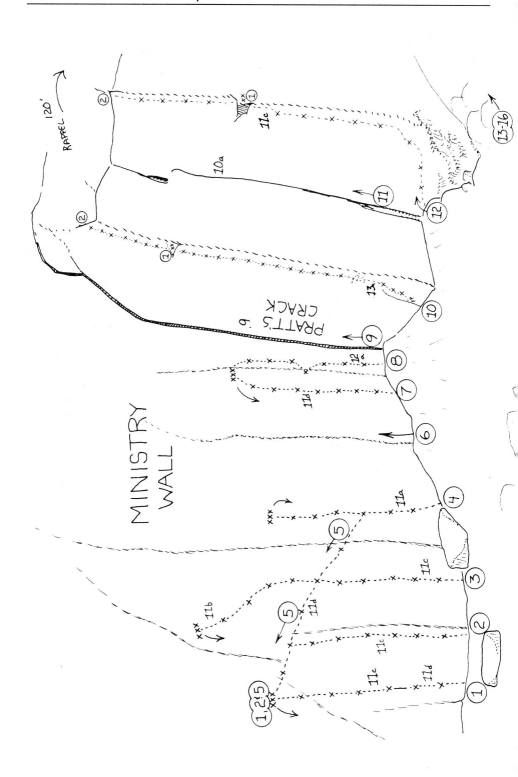

Ministry Wall

This is the vertical face to the left of Pratt's Crack (an off-width crack in a large corner). One rope is sufficient to lower off all routes.

1 *Twitch* 5.11c/d ★★ Pro: 6 bolts.
2 *Effigy* 5.11a/b ★★ Pro: 8 bolts.
3 *Burning Inside* 5.11c ★★ Pro: 10 bolts.
4 *Stigmata* 5.10d/11a ★★ Pro: 6 bolts.
5 *Flashback* 5.11d/12a ★ Pro: 8 bolts. Start on Stigmata, go left from third bolt, crossing Burning Inside and Effigy to finish atop Twitch.
6 *Project*
7 *New World Order* 5.11c/d ★★ Pro: 7 bolts.
8 *Deity* 5.12a/b ★ Pro: 7 bolts.

Routes Right of Pratt's Crack

As the name implies, all the following routes lie on the rock to the right (and around the corner) from Pratt's Crack (the obvious off-width in the large dihedral).

9 *Pratt's Crack* 5.9 ★★ Classic off-width (is there such a thing?) 2 pitches. Descend off to the right (rappel). Pro: To 8 inches.
10 *Ecstasy* 5.13a ★★★ The obvious and wild arête right of Pratt's Crack. 2 pitches. Pitch 1 Pro: 16 bolts, 1 fixed pin (125 feet). Pitch 2: 12b/c. Pro: 8 bolts.
11 *Sheila* 5.10a ★★ The hand crack in the corner just right of Ecstasy. Descend off to the right (rappel). Pro: To 3.5 inches.
12 *Eclipsed* 5.11c ★★ 2 pitches. Start from beginning of Sheila, traverse up and right to the arête. Follow the arête. Pro, Pitch 1: 8 bolts; Pitch 2: 4 bolts.
13 *Wind in the Willows* 5.11c/d (or 5.12d) ★★★ Starts just around the corner from Eclipsed. Most parties do the first 80 feet of this route and lower (5.11c/d; Pro: 8 bolts). However, you can continue past 4 more bolts for a distinctly more difficult adventure (5.12d; 115 feet).
14 *Planetarium* 5.12a ★ Pro: 7 bolts. On face right of Wind In The Willows.
15 *Atomic Gecko* 5.12a ★★ Next route to the right of Planetarium. Pro: 5 bolts.
16 *Biohazard* 5.12b ★★ Just right of Atomic Gecko. Pro: 5 bolts.

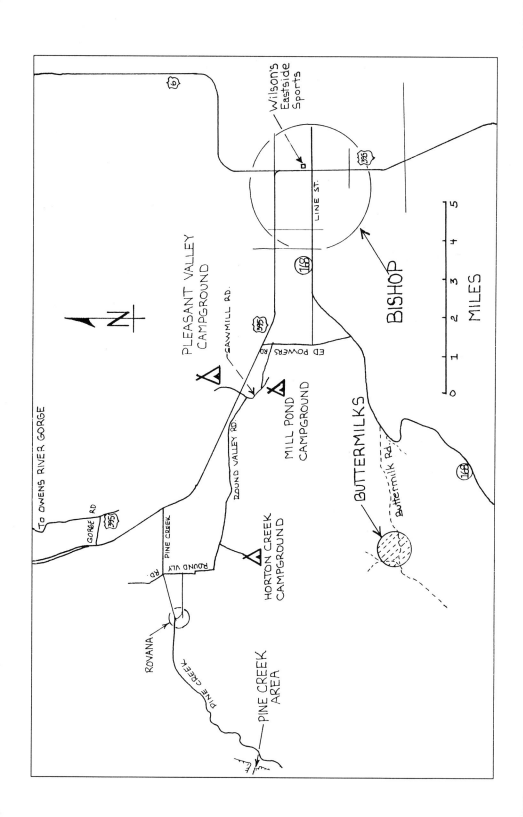

The Buttermilks

These large granite boulders are located just outside Bishop and offer high-off-the-deck overhanging problems. Most problems are done without a top-rope; few anchors are found on top. The exception to this rule are the giant Grandma and Grandpa Peabody Boulders, which have bolt anchors. It is advisable to check out descents before you ascend a problem (you may be climbing up the route which is also your descent!) Climbers visiting Owens River Gorge find The Buttermilks a nice diversion and sometimes camp here.

How to get to the Buttermilks
From Highway 395 in Bishop, turn west onto Line Street (Highway 168). Follow Highway 168 to Buttermilk Road (dirt); turn right here. About 3.4 miles from Highway 168, you pass a large parking area on your right; park here or continue a bit further and park alongside the road. The Boulders will be seen on your right.

Equipment
Shoes, chalkbag, and perhaps a short rope (100-foot).

Season
The Buttermilks enjoy a long season, and except for the hottest days of summer or coldest days of winter, should be climbable.

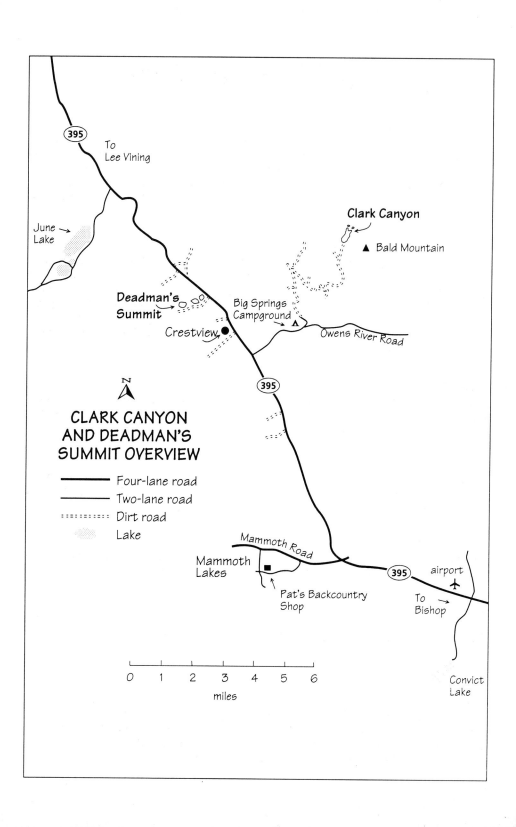

395
To
Lee Vining

June →
Lake

Clark Canyon

▲ Bald Mountain

**Deadman's
Summit**

Big Springs
Campground

Crestview ●

Owens River Road

N

**CLARK CANYON
AND DEADMAN'S
SUMMIT OVERVIEW**

────── Four-lane road
────── Two-lane road
:::::::::: Dirt road
▒▒▒ Lake

395

Mammoth Road

Mammoth
Lakes ■

395   airport
✈

Pat's Backcountry
Shop

To →
Bishop

0   1   2   3   4   5   6

miles

Convict
Lake

Clark Canyon Crags

Clark Canyon offers short, fun sport climbs on highly-pocketed volcanic rock in a scenic remote locale. Popular primarily with local climbers, its closeness to Owens River Gorge and Mammoth Lakes make it worth a visit. Several other crags in the vicinity have also been developed. The rock tends to be a little friable, but routes are generally well protected (a few are a little runout). There is a good selection of sport-type routes from easy 5.10 to 5.12a.

How to get to Clark Canyon

From Highway 395, take Owens River Road east for about 2 miles (Owens River Road is located about 7 miles north of the Mammoth Lakes exit and 17 miles south of Lee Vining) to Big Springs Campground (on your left). Turn left here, and then immediately take the road to the right of the campground entrance (this turns to dirt after a few hundred yards). A myriad of dirt roads are followed to the parking area. See maps on pages 32 and 35. Be sure to close both cattle gates/fences behind you. A short (10 minute) hike takes you to the base of the rock.

Equipment

Bring quickdraws and a few rappel slings (not all anchors have shuts). Most climbs require only one rope to descend. A rope-bag/tarp is recommended, as the base is quite dirty. A few climbs (not recommended) may need conventional gear.

Season

Clark Canyon is located at 8,000 feet and is primarily a late spring to fall climbing area. Nevertheless, it can be quite warm in the sun, and afternoons provide good shade to routes on the southeastern face. Small insects and mosquitoes can be bothersome.

Guidebooks

Mammoth Area Sport Climbs by John Moynier and Marty Lewis has complete route info on Clark Canyon and several other areas near Mammoth Lakes.

Local Climbing Shops

Pat's Backcountry Shop, located in the Sherwin Professional Plaza on Old Mammoth Road (0.25 mile south of Meridian Blvd.), Mammoth Lakes, CA. (619) 934-2008.

Climbing Routes

The following routes lie on the southern side of the main crag, and get afternoon shade. These routes all face Bald Mountain. A number of other routes lie on the western side and further uphill from the routes shown. Also, good bouldering can be found northwest of the main crag, and on the Holy Boulder, which lies up the gully on the northwestern side of the main formation.

**Clark Canyon Crag
South Face**

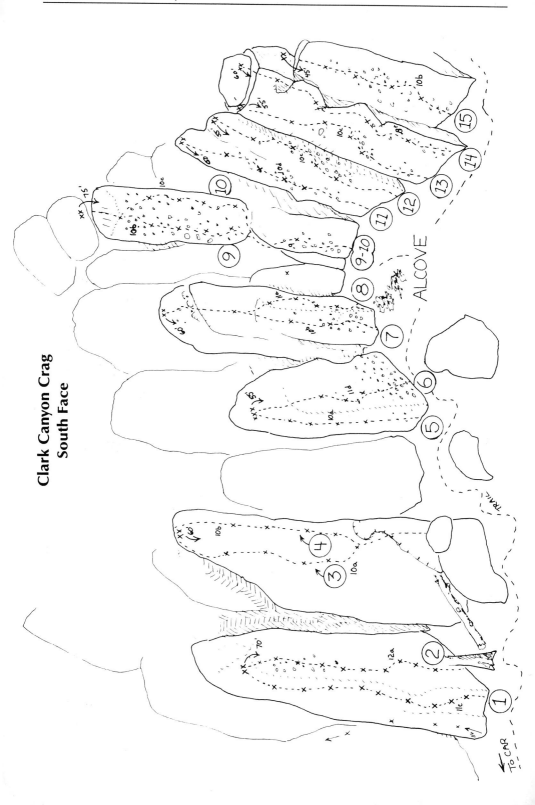

 1 *Jihad* 5.11c ★★ Pro: 9 bolts.
 2 *Dirty Dancing* 5.12a ★★ Pro: 10 bolts.
 3 *Welcome to Bohemia* 5.10a Pro: 5 bolts.
 4 *Rocket In My Pocket* 5.10b R ★★ Pro: 5 bolts.
 5 *Wholly Cow* 5.10a Pro: 4 bolts.
 6 *El Toro* 5.11d ★ Pro: 3 bolts.
 7 *Unknown* 5.10b R Pro: 3 bolts (anchor in awkward location).
 8 *Tickled Pink* 5.11a ★★ Pro: 5 bolts (anchor in awkward location).
 9 *Dr. Jekyll* 5.10a/b ★★ Pro: 6 bolts.
10 *Mr. Hyde* 5.10c Pro: 6 bolts.
11 *Craters* 5.10d Pro: 4 bolts.
12 *Eightball* 5.10c ★ Pro: 4 bolts.
13 *Pickpocket* 5.10c Pro: 4 bolts (rap off/no descent rigs for lowering).
14 *Stegosaurus* 5.9- ★ Pro: 4 bolts.
15 *Pocket Pool* 5.10b ★ Pro: 4 bolts.

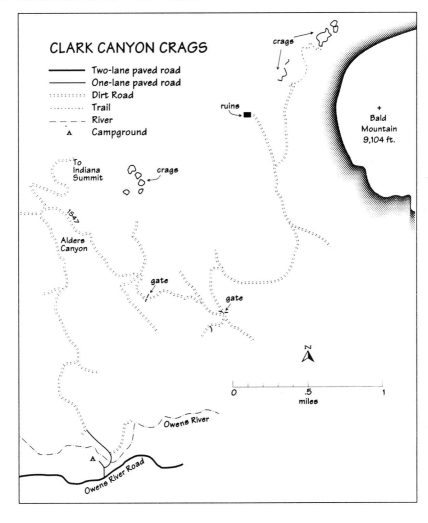

Kevin Powell

Mike Waugh on Grandpa Peabody, The Buttermilks

Deadman's Summit

This excellent bouldering spot is located just west of Highway 395 approximately 10 miles north of the Mammoth Lakes exit, and about 14.5 miles south of Lee Vining (1.1 miles south of Bald Mountain Road). (See map page 32.) The crags consist of solid volcanic rock pockmarked with many pockets and features. An unmarked dirt road heads west and gives access to several south-facing boulders/short cliffs. The first area is located near Highway 395; two other areas are found 0.4 mile and 0.2 mile farther along the dirt road. Problems can range up to 30 feet (above a soft pumice base); a top-rope may be useful for some of the problems. Care should be taken not to drive too far off established roads. Many cars have gotten stuck in the soft pumice.

Season
Spring through late fall. 8,000 foot elevation means snow in the winter.

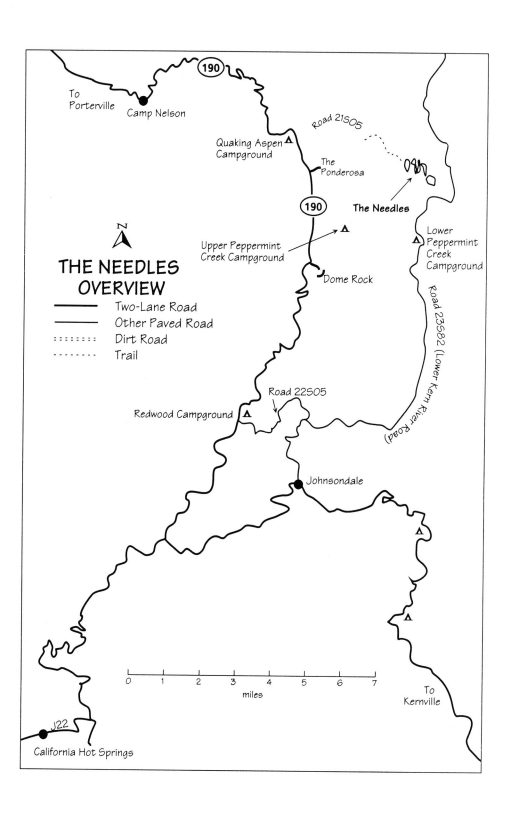

190

To
Porterville
Camp Nelson

Road 21S05

Quaking Aspen ▲
Campground

The
Ponderosa

190

The Needles

Upper Peppermint ▲
Creek Campground

Lower ▲
Peppermint
Creek
Campground

Dome Rock

N

THE NEEDLES
OVERVIEW
———— Two-Lane Road
———— Other Paved Road
:::::::: Dirt Road
-------- Trail

Road 23S82 (Lower Kern River Road)

Road 22S05

Redwood Campground ▲

Johnsondale

▲

▲

0   1   2   3   4   5   6   7
miles

To
Kernville

J22
California Hot Springs

The Needles

The Needles of the southern Sierra Nevada have a long climbing history and offer arguably the best granite climbing in the United States. It is not to be confused with the far better known Needles of South Dakota. Perhaps its somewhat remote location and (until recently) lack of route information explain its relative obscurity.

The rock is unglaciated granite and unsurpassed in quality. The "needle" and dome-like formations offer often intimidating climbs up to 12 pitches long, but most average 3 to 5 rope-lengths. There is a good mixture of both face climbing (slabs to some steeper stuff) to incredible crack routes. The 2.5-mile hike puts you in the middle of awesome mountain scenery.

No toilet facilities are available at the trailhead (or the rocks), so care should be taken to bury human waste at least 6 inches, and please be sure to pack used toilet paper out in a resealable plastic bag. Nearby Dome Rock also offers multi-pitch slab climbing with an easy approach.

Also be aware that peregrine falcons (an endangered species) have been seen in The Needles area. These birds are sensitive to disturbance, particularly during late January to July. Avoid climbing near nesting sites. If you encounter a peregrine while climbing (usually it dive-bombs you), retreat or quickly finish the climb (whatever takes the least time).

How to get to The Needles

From the north
Take Highway 99 south to Highway 190 (to Porterville) passing Camp Nelson to Forest Service Road 21S05 (on the left).

From the east
From Highway 14 (just south of the Highway 395/Highway 14 interchange) head west on Highway 178 to Lake Isabella. Head north through Kernville along the Kern River, then turn left (west) at Johnsondale on the California Hot Springs/Parker Pass Road. After about 7 miles, turn north on Highway 190 (past the Ponderosa) to Forest Service Road 21S05 (on the right).

From the south/Los Angeles
Most climbers take US 5 north to Highway 99. Follow Highway 99 north past Bakersfield to the exit for the town of Earlimart, head east to California Hot Springs, then join Highway 190 north (past the Ponderosa) to Forest Service Road 21S05 (on the right). It may be easier to take Highway 14 to Highway 178 (See "From the east" above) from the southeast (i.e. Joshua Tree).

From the Highway 190/Road 21S05 intersection

Head east on Road 21S05 (dirt road; closed approximately November to May) for about 3 miles to its end, where there is a parking area. Road 21S05 is marked by a "Needles Lookout" sign.

Follow the trail east to The Needles (2.5 miles) which ends at the base of stairs leading to the fire lookout atop the Magician Dome. From the stairs, head northeast and downhill, and cross low-angle slabs. Trail markers lead down to the climbing areas. Plan on 1 to 1.5 hours to hike to the climbs (Sorcerer/Witch Gully).

Season

The Needles is best visited during the late spring to early fall (May to October). Be aware that Forest Service Road 21S05 may be closed depending on weather conditions and the amount of snow remaining (or early snowfall).

Equipment

The Needles is primarily a "traditional" climbing area, which means that you should take a fair amount of gear, including multiples of camming devices in each size. Two ropes are recommended to facilitate easy rappels/retreats. It should also be noted that there are a number of sparsely-protected face routes, and care should be taken before starting up a face climb that you know little about. Some of the harder face climbs are well-bolted, however.

Guidebooks

The Needles Area, Southern Sierra Rock Climbing, Book 2, by Moser, Vernon and Paul provides comprehensive route information for The Needles, Dome Rock and a multitude of other crags in the vicinity. If you plan an extended stay or regular visits, it is recommended. It can be purchased at most climbing stores.

Camping

Camping is unrestricted in the National Forest lands near The Needles and many people camp at the trailhead (end of Road 21S05). Maintained campgrounds include: Peppermint Campground (near Dome Rock, off Highway 190, south of Road 21S05) also offers free camping. Quaking Aspen Campground (off Highway 190, just north of Road 21S05) offers potable water and charges Forest Service Rates. The Ponderosa (on Highway 190, south of Road 21S05) offers lodging; reservations may be required.

Local Climbing Shops

Bigfoot Mountaineering
2500 New Stine Road
Bakersfield, CA
(805) 834-4314

Bill Freeman

In The Needles

Mountain High, Ltd.
123 Diamond Peak
Ridgecrest, CA 93555
(619) 375-2612
(800) 255-3182

Sierra South
11300 Kernville Road
Kernville, CA
(619) 376-3745

Rescue Information

The Tulare County Sheriff is responsible for rescues at The Needles. They may be reached by dialing 911 or (714) 376-6400. Nevertheless, climbers should, as a general rule, take responsibility for their own rescues when practical.

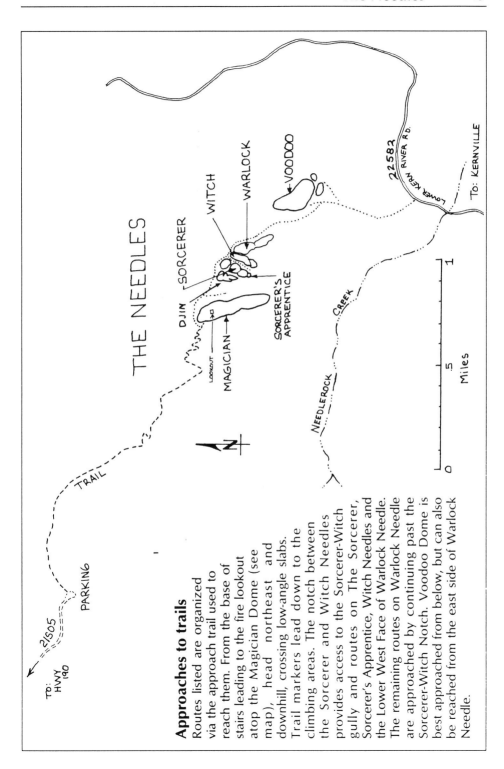

Approaches to trails

Routes listed are organized via the approach trail used to reach them. From the base of stairs leading to the fire lookout atop the Magician Dome (see map), head northeast and downhill, crossing low-angle slabs. Trail markers lead down to the climbing areas. The notch between the Sorcerer and Witch Needles provides access to the Sorcerer-Witch gully and routes on The Sorcerer, Sorcerer's Apprentice, Witch Needles and the Lower West Face of Warlock Needle. The remaining routes on Warlock Needle are approached by continuing past the Sorcerer-Witch Notch. Voodoo Dome is best approached from below, but can also be reached from the east side of Warlock Needle.

Sorcerer East Face

The East Face of the Sorcerer has many of the finest crack climbs in The Needles (if not the entire United States).

Lower East Face

The following routes start atop a pinnacle of rock below and right of the main East Face. Scramble down the gully between Sorcerer and Witch, past the Fire Wall. The top of the pinnacle is reached by climbing a 5.7 chimney on its right side (just left of the Fire Wall).

1   ***Davy Jones Locker*** 5.12b ★★★ Start on the left side top of the pinnacle, in the right-hand of two cracks (in a shallow right-facing corner); climb this over a roof to difficult face climbing. 2-bolt belay/rap. Pro: Bring several 1.5 to 2.5 inches.
2   ***Pieces of Eight*** 5.12c ★★ The hand and finger crack on the right. 2-bolt anchor/rap. Pro: To: 2.5 inches.

East Face

The main East Face is reached by scrambling down the Sorcerer-Witch gully, then out along a large ledge system atop the Fire Wall.

Descent: Rappel (110 feet to notch, or 80 feet to Class 4 downclimbing) from a 2-bolt anchor on the right side of the summit.

3   ***The Avenger*** 5.13a/b Up the corner then left to the Pieces of Eight belay. Pro: 6 bolts, thin gear.
4   ***Wailing Banshees*** 5.11a/b ★★ The long left-facing corner. Pro: To 3 inches.
5   ***Scirocco*** 5.11d/12a ★★★ The arête to the right of Wailing Banshees. Pro: 15 bolts.
6   ***Don Juan Wall*** 5.11b ★★★ Start as per Thin Ice, but go left to reach the crack and corner system. Pro: Thin to 2.5 inches.
7   ***Thin Ice*** 5.10b ★★★ A classic. Pro: Thin to 3 inches.
8   ***Atlantis*** 5.11c ★★★ Pro: Many thin to 2.5 inches.

Fire Wall

Scramble down the Sorcerer-Witch gully, continue down until you are just below the ledge where the East Face routes start. The Fire Wall is characterized by the bright yellow lichen on the face. The following routes require thin pro, or can be top-roped from bolts above.

9   ***Spontaneous Combustion*** 5.12c/d ★★
10 ***Pyrotechnics*** 5.12 c/d ★★
11 ***Pyromania*** 5.13a ★★★

**Sorcerer East Face
and Fire Wall**

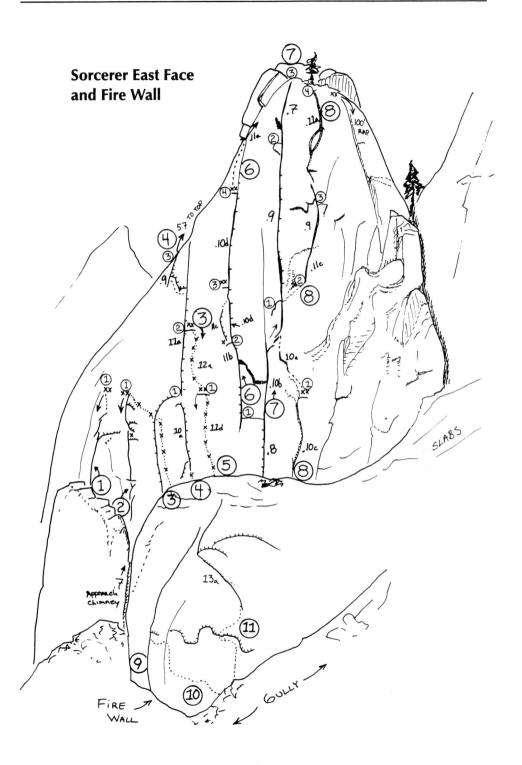

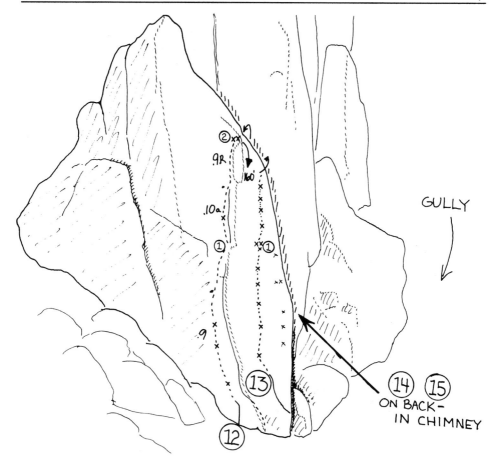

Sorcerer's Apprentice

This 350-foot pinnacle of rock lies at the very bottom of the Sorcerer-Witch gully, on the west side (the Sorcerer side). It is the lowest formation, leaning up against the formations above.

Approach: Either descend the Sorcerer-Witch gully, or go down the gully between Magician and Djin along a steep trail.

South Face

Descent: Rappel down Love Potion #9. (Two 165-foot ropes needed.)

   12 *Broomsticks* 5.10a ★★ Pro: Thin to 2 inches, runners.
   13 *Love Potion #9* 5.10b ★★ Pro: To 2 inches, runners.

Northeast Face

To reach the following routes, climb a fourth-class chimney in a deep recess on the overhanging right side of the formation. The following routes start out of this recess.

   14 *Piranha* 5.12c ★★★ The 6-bolt route on the left; 2-bolt anchor/rap.
   15 *Parasite* 5.13b ★★ This is the 12-bolt climb on the right leading to a 2-bolt anchor/rap.

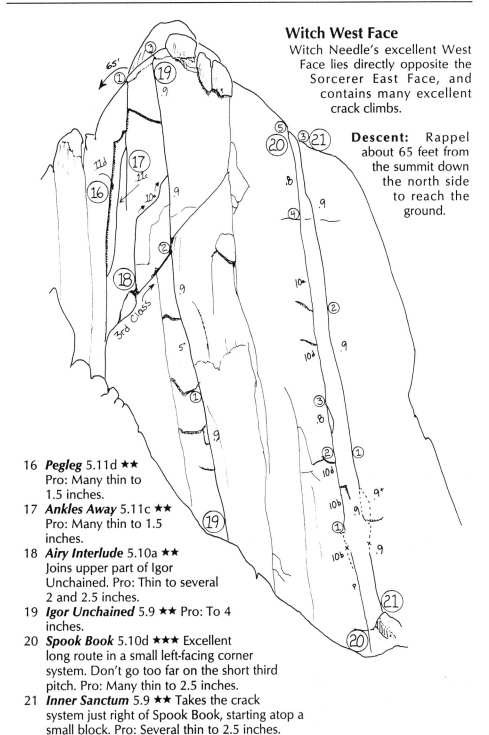

Witch West Face

Witch Needle's excellent West Face lies directly opposite the Sorcerer East Face, and contains many excellent crack climbs.

Descent: Rappel about 65 feet from the summit down the north side to reach the ground.

16 **Pegleg** 5.11d ★★ Pro: Many thin to 1.5 inches.

17 **Ankles Away** 5.11c ★★ Pro: Many thin to 1.5 inches.

18 **Airy Interlude** 5.10a ★★ Joins upper part of Igor Unchained. Pro: Thin to several 2 and 2.5 inches.

19 **Igor Unchained** 5.9 ★★ Pro: To 4 inches.

20 **Spook Book** 5.10d ★★★ Excellent long route in a small left-facing corner system. Don't go too far on the short third pitch. Pro: Many thin to 2.5 inches.

21 **Inner Sanctum** 5.9 ★★ Takes the crack system just right of Spook Book, starting atop a small block. Pro: Several thin to 2.5 inches.

Warlock Lower West Face

The Lower West Face of Warlock Needle is best reached by scrambling all the way down the Sorcerer-Witch Gully, then heading east below the lowest formation (called Necromancer), then back up the gully on the other side. Romantic Warrior lies in the huge, sweeping, left-facing dihedral; Sea of Tranquility takes the arête on the right (formed by the dihedral).

Descent: Rap off the north side of Warlock Needle. Two rappels (120-foot and 135-foot) from the summit down The Howling. Bring two ropes.

22 *Romantic Warrior* 5.12b ★★★ This 1,000-foot route is one of the mega-classics of long, hard crack routes. Pro: Many of all sizes (thin to 2.5+).

23 *Sea of Tranquility* 5.12b ★★★ Climb the first pitch of Romantic Warrior, then traverse right to the amazing arête. After 4 pitches, join Romantic Warrior; continue up that route, or rap off from here (2 ropes needed).

Warlock Needle

The remaining routes on Warlock Needle are best reached by continuing along the trail (east) past the Sorcerer-Witch Notch. The Upper West Face routes are easily reached from the trail as it runs along the north end of the formation. To reach the East Face routes, continue around to the east side, and down along the base.

Upper West Face

Walk past the Sorcerer-Witch Notch to the north side of Warlock (just past Witch North Face, a rock "notch" connects the Witch and Warlock north faces). The Warlock north face has two parallel hand cracks that end atop blocks; this is the first pitch of The Howling. To reach The Titanic and The Spell, do the first pitch of the Howling, then a short rappel leads to the base of these routes.

Descent: Two rappels (120-foot and 135-foot) from the summit down The Howling (bring two ropes).

24 *The Howling* 5.10a ★ Climb either crack (see above; the left-hand is better), continue up and left on face climbing past bolts to the top. Pro: To 2.5 inches.

25 *The Titanic* 5.12c ★★★ Begin in a right-facing corner with a wide crack, then up the bolt-protected face to the top. Pro: A few large, bolts.

26 *The Spell* 5.10a ★ This is the very obvious, wide crack down and right of The Titanic. Pro: Many large to 5 inches.

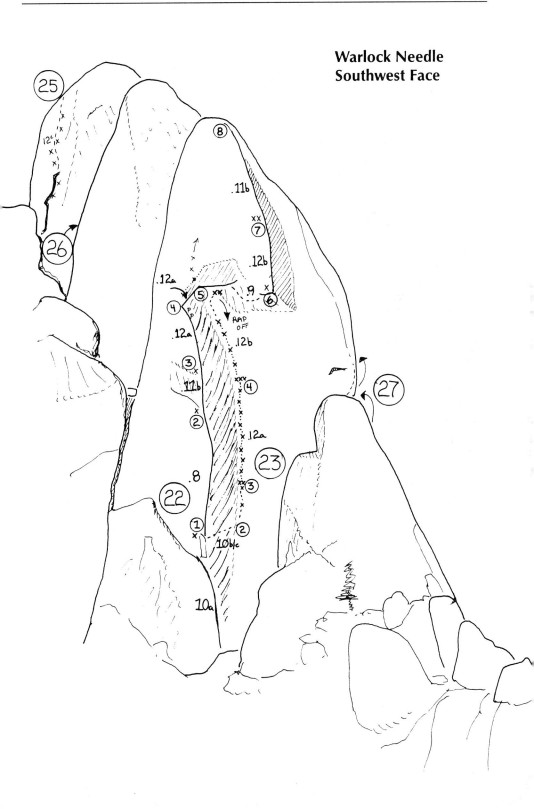

Warlock Needle
Southwest Face

Warlock East Face

Warlock East Face

Hike down the east side of the formation.

Descent: From the summit block, two double-rope rappels down north face for South Face Route. See topos for other descents.

27 *South Face Route* 5.9 or 5.10c ★★ Start downhill from the clean face in a vegetated gully. Climb the left-hand series of cracks to a pine tree. More cracks lead to a large ledge. Above, face and crack climbing lead to a chimney system and the summit. Pro: Several thin to 3 inches.

28 *Giant Steps* 5.10c ★ Most people rappel after second pitch (160 feet; bring two ropes). Pro: Quickdraws, a thin nut or two.

29 *A Gathering of Wolves* 5.10d ★ Joins Giant Steps, 160-foot rappel off.

30 *Planet Waves* 5.11a ★ Traverse left and downclimb north side (some may make a short rappel). Pro: Several thin to 2 inches.

31 *Imaginary Voyage* 5.9- ★ Either descend off to the left after 2 pitches or continue to the top and make 2 rappels from the summit (2 ropes needed). Pro: To 2.5 inches.

Mike Waugh on *Ankles Away*, 5.11c, Witch Needle

Voodoo Dome

This 900-foot dome lies on the far eastern part of the granite domes and formations of The Needles. It can be best reached from Lower Needlerock Creek, off Forest Service Road 23S82 (about 1 hour uphill on a trail). Take Highway 190 to Road 22S05 to Road 23S82, then north until below Voodoo Dome. It can also be reached from the east side of Warlock Needle, but this is more of a bushwhack and takes longer. See map page 38.

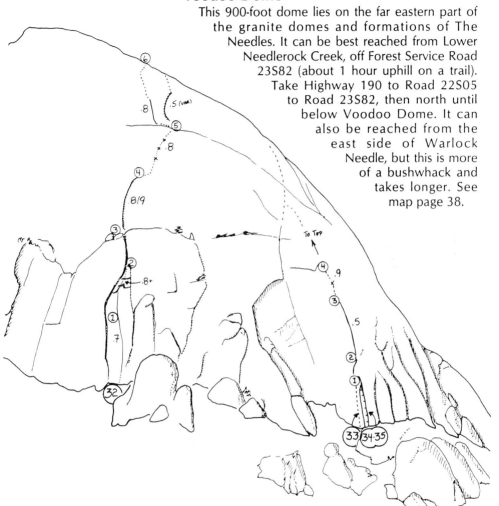

32 **White Punks on Dope** 5.8+ ★★★ 6 Pitches. Start in a straight-in crack just right of a right-facing corner system. After 2 pitches join the corner system to a ledge. Above, climb a left-facing corner to a belay. A face climbing pitch (somewhat runout) past 3 bolts leads to another ledge system. A 5.8 crack and face pitch to the left leads to the top. Pro: Thin to 3 inches.

33 **Millennium Falcon** 5.13b ★★ Start left of the Pea Soup/Dark Side dihedral; face climb past 4 bolts to a 2-bolt belay. Above, climb up to an arête, then past more bolts to a bolt belay. Rappel from here. Pro: Thin and quickdraws.

34 **Pea Soup** 5.11b/c ★★ Climb the fingers to hand crack on the left-hand face of the dihedral system. Pro: Thin to 2.5 inches.

35 **The Dark Side** 5.12c ★★ Climb the crack in the corner. Joins with Pea Soup. Pro: Thin to 2.5 inches.

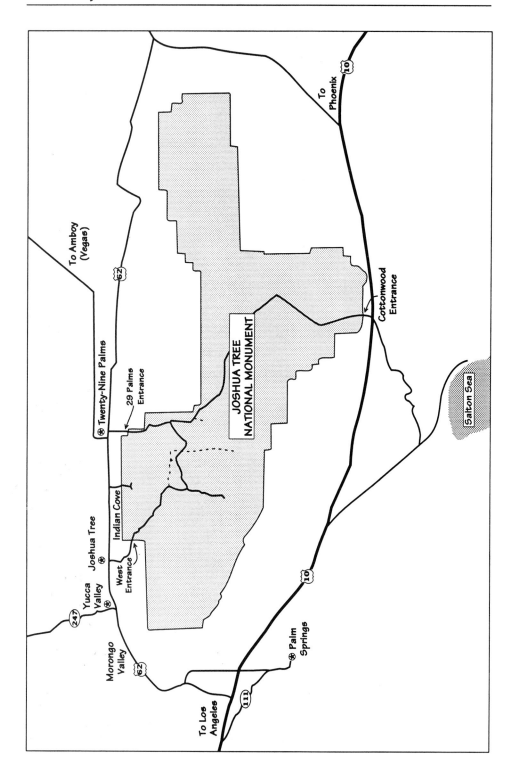

Joshua Tree National Monument

There are over 4,000 established routes at Joshua Tree. It is one of the most popular climbing areas in the United States. A selection of over 200 of these routes is included in this guide. The rock at Joshua Tree is a rough-textured granite. Formations tend to be dome-like, and in most cases are surrounded by flat sandy washes and open plains. Many formations have a number of boulders around their base which can offer excellent boulder problems.

The cracks at Joshua Tree are plentiful and vary from shallow and flared to clean and split. Camming devices are extremely helpful (and often necessary), and provide protection in flared or horizontal cracks that are commonly seen in the Monument. It is not uncommon for the rock at Joshua Tree to vary considerably in quality; ranging from quite grainy and even loose to extreme high quality and smooth. However, as a general rule, the rock tends to be relatively sound.

How to get to Joshua Tree
Joshua Tree National Monument is located in the high desert of eastern southern California, approximately 140 miles east of Los Angeles and about 35 miles northeast of Palm Springs.

From Southern California
Take the quickest route to Interstate 10, head east past the Palm Springs Exit (Highway 111), taking the US 62 Exit North (toward 29 Palms). Several uphill grades take you through Morongo Valley to Yucca Valley. Several miles past Yucca Valley is the town of Joshua Tree. Turn right (south) on Quail Springs Road which leads directly to the Monument Entrance some 5 miles up the road.

From the East (through Las Vegas)
Approximately 55 miles west of Las Vegas (on Interstate 15), there is a particularly good shortcut directly toward 29 Palms, via the railroad towns of Cima and Kelso, past the Granite Mountains, crossing Interstate 40, then past Amboy to 29 Palms. However, this road is extremely desolate and a few miles follow a well-graded dirt road. The alternative (normal route) is to take Interstate 15 to Barstow and take Highway 247 south until it terminates in Yucca Valley (see above).

From the Bay Area and the Pacific Northwest
From the San Francisco Bay Area and Pacific Northwest, head south via either Interstate 5 or Highway 99 to Bakersfield. From Bakersfield take Highway 58 east to Barstow (Highway 58 turns into Interstate 40). From Barstow, take Highway 247 south to Lucerne Valley, and continue on Highway 247 to Yucca Valley (see above).

Old Woman Springs Road is Highway 247 where it intersects Highway 62 (29 Palms Highway) in Yucca Valley.

From the Southwest
From the southwestern part of the United States (Arizona, New Mexico, etc.), one can take US 10 west to the southern (Cottonwood) entrance to the Monument near the City of Indio. Alternatively, one can take Interstate 40 west, then head south to Amboy and eventually to 29 Palms.

Via Airline or Bus
Other climbers may, for practical reasons, make their initial "approach" via commercial airline to either the Los Angeles Area or Palm Springs. Although a rental car is helpful in getting about in the Monument, it is not a necessity. Bus transport from Palm Springs (about 35 miles southwest of the Monument) to the towns of Yucca Valley, Joshua Tree and 29 Palms is via Desert Stageline: (619) 367-3581. The Desert Stageline Bus leaves both Palm Springs Airport and the Palm Springs Greyhound Bus Terminal three times daily.

Entrance Fees
The National Parks Service imposes an entrance (user) fee of $5 per vehicle (good for 7 days). For $15 you can buy a "Joshua Tree" yearly pass (good January 1 to December 31), good only at Joshua Tree National Monument). The best bet is a Golden Eagle Pass ($25); may be used at all National Parks/Monuments (good January 1 to December 31).

Season
The season starts in early to mid-October and extends to late April or early May. The best months for climbing are usually late October to early December and March through April. Temperatures *may* be climbable (in the shade) even during the summer.

Equipment
Bring a good selection of gear, from quickdraws to camming devices. Top-roping is common, so extension slings are helpful. A 165-foot (50-meter) rope should be sufficient. Even bolted face routes may require some gear.

Guidebooks
Joshua Tree Rock Climbing Guide, Second Edition, by Randy Vogel is the only comprehensive guide. *Joshua Tree Bouldering Guide* by Mari Gingery is also recommended. Alan Bartlett has produced a series of smaller guides to some of the individual areas in the Monument.

Climbing Shops
There are two climbing shops near the Monument:

Cottonwood Camping
6376 Adobe Road
29 Palms, CA 92277
(619) 367-9505

Nomad Ventures
61325 29 Palms Highway #A
Joshua Tree, CA 92252
(619) 366-4684.

Camping

The Monument has several campgrounds, five of which climbers will be interested in: Hidden Valley, Ryan, Jumbo, Belle and Indian Cove. On many weekends, all of these are congested. Since there is no fee for most of the camping, there is no means of reserving a campsite. There is a 14 days per year camping limit in the Monument. Because of the popularity of Hidden Valley Campground, this is where most camping limit problems arise.

There are virtually no formal car camping areas outside the Monument. The sole exception is Knott's Sky Park in 29 Palms (which is primarily a RV park). Rates are approximately $7.50 per day.

To contact the Visitors' Center: (619) 367-7511. To contact the Monument Headquarters: (619) 367-6376.

Motel Accommodations

Many climbers who travel long distances to the Monument for short visits may not have all their camping gear with them, or find that all the campgrounds are full. For these and other reasons it is common for climbers to stay in one of the many reasonably-priced motels in the Yucca Valley and 29 Palms area.

Eating

There is no water or food available in the Monument. Either stock up before entering the Monument or have a car at your disposal for this purpose. The nearby town of Yucca Valley has several well-stocked, modern supermarkets. Additionally, the towns of Yucca Valley, Joshua Tree and 29 Palms have a virtual swarm of reasonably-priced restaurants, as well as fast food places.

Campfires

Bring wood with you (it can also be purchased in town). *No* natural vegetation (dead or not) may be gathered for burning or any other purpose in the Monument. The desert ecology depends upon the natural decay of plant life. In addition to being an environmentally unsound practice, it is illegal; you can be cited by the rangers and fined.

Showers

Showers are available at Lee's Health Club in Yucca Valley. Lee's is located about five blocks west of Denny's at 56460 29 Palms Highway, Yucca Valley. Lee's telephone number is: (619) 365-9402.

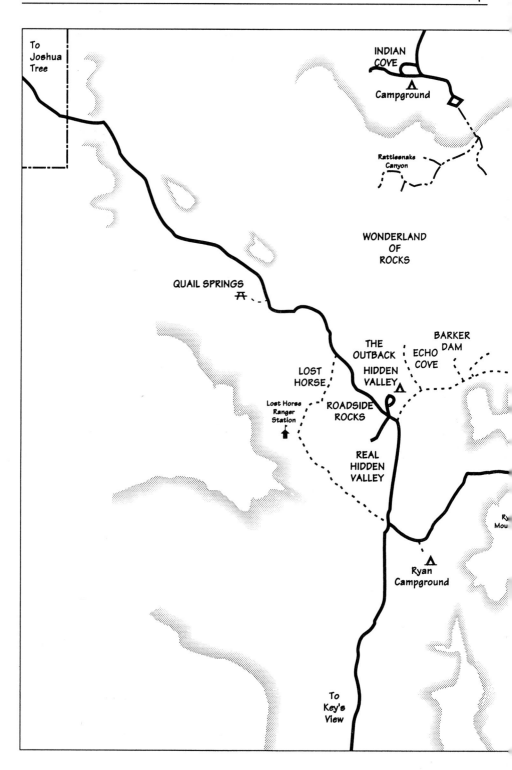

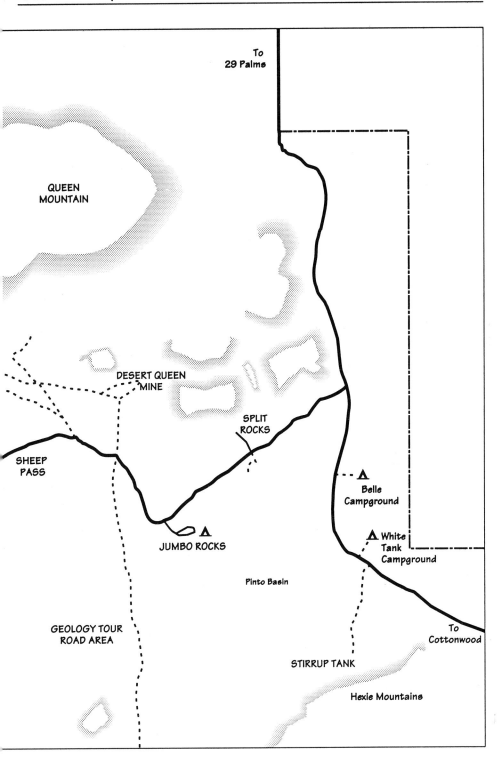

To
29 Palms

QUEEN
MOUNTAIN

DESERT QUEEN
MINE

SPLIT
ROCKS

SHEEP
PASS

Belle
Campground

White
Tank
Campground

JUMBO ROCKS

Pinto Basin

GEOLOGY TOUR
ROAD AREA

To
Cottonwood

STIRRUP TANK

Hexie Mountains

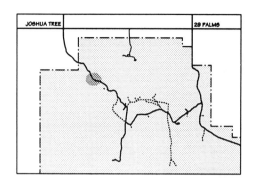

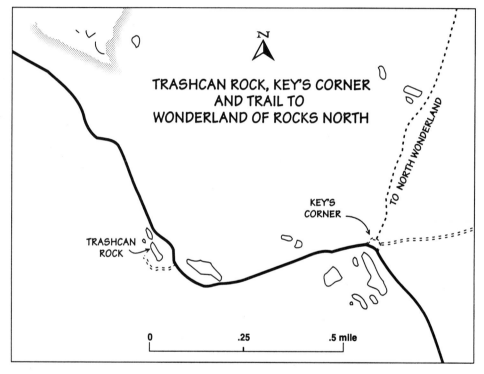

Trashcan Rock (Quail Springs Picnic Area)

Trashcan Rock is the first formation of major importance encountered on the drive into the Monument from the town of Joshua Tree. A paved parking area, picnic table and bathroom are found here, but no camping is allowed. The Park Service has designated this area for day-use only. This is a fine beginners' area. Trashcan Rock is located on the right (west) side of the road, approximately 6 miles from the park entrance.

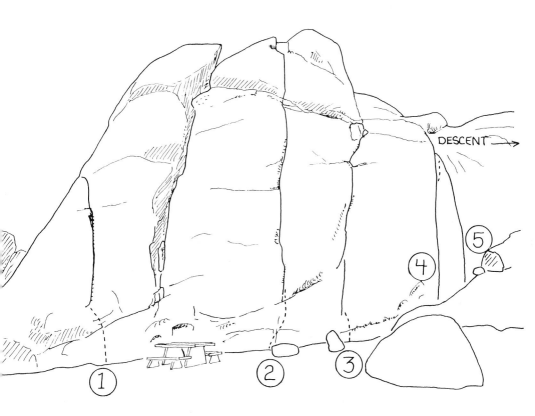

Trashcan Rock East Face

Easiest descent is off the north end of the formation.

1 **Ripper** 5.11   Boulder problem.
2 **Hermeneutic** 5.10c R ★   Thin and hard to protect at crux. Pro: Mostly small to 2 inches.
3 **Butterfly Crack** 5.11c ★★ The classic on the formation. Start with a boulder problem-like crux at the bottom, which leads to easier (5.9) climbing. Pro: Small wired nuts to 2.5 inches.
4 **Left Sawdust Crack** 5.10c   Usually top-roped; crux at the top. Pro: Small to 2 inches.
5 **Right Sawdust Crack** 5.8 ★   Hand crack. Pro: Medium to 2.5 inches.

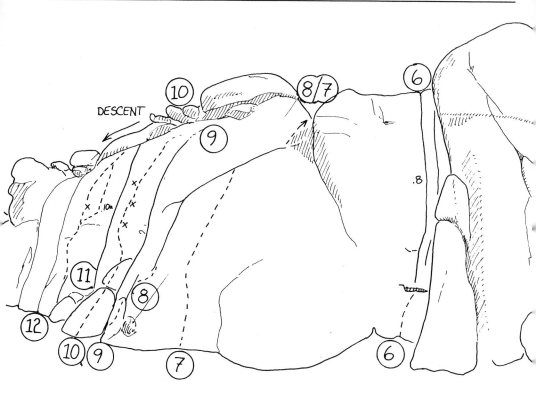

Trashcan Rock West Face

Many of the face routes (with exception of Tiptoe and Profundity) are unprotected and usually top-roped. Descend off the north end of the rock.

  6 *Cranny* 5.8 ★   A fun route up double cracks. Pro: To 2 inches.
  7 *Baby-Point-Five*   5.8 R/X   Hard entry moves (unprotected) to easy crack-ramp.
  8 *Walkway* 5.4 R   Unprotected crux at bottom.
  9 *B-1* 5.1   Pro: To 3 inches.
 10 *Tiptoe* 5.7+ ★   Fun route past 3 bolts.
 11 *B-2* 5.3   Pro: To 3 inches.
 12 *Profundity* 5.10a (or 5.10c) Pro: 2 bolts. Going straight up past the bolt is more difficult than going slightly right, then up.

Wonderland of Rocks North

The Wonderland of Rocks constitutes the largest concentration of rock formations in the entire monument. This area (in excess of nine square miles) is bounded by Indian Cove to the north, Barker Dam to the south, Key's Ranch to the west and Queen Mountain to the east. Due to its vast size, exploration has been divided by two separate points of entry. For this reason, the Wonderland is treated in two different sections. The northern section (Wonderland North) and areas within the vicinity of the approach trail are described here (see map for coverage). The southern section (Wonderland South) is described near the Barker Dam section.

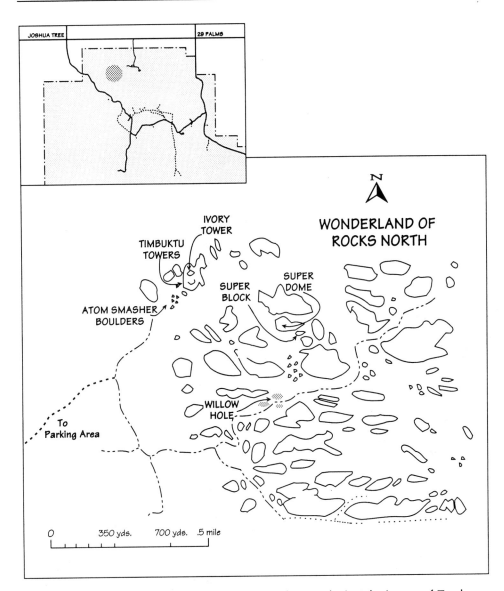

At Key's Corner (a sharp right turn in the road 0.7 mile (1.1 km) east of Trashcan Rock; approximately 6.7 miles from the monument entrance), there is a parking area (Key's Corner Parking). Wonderland North and all other areas described in this section are approached via a trail (the Wonderland Trail) that heads northeast from the Key's Corner parking lot. About 1 mile from Key's Corner parking area, the Wonderland Trail joins a larger north-south trail (the Old Trail). Head north. After 350 yards, you will pass the junction of the Wonderland/Old Trail with the Indian Cove hiking trail (don't take the Indian Cove Trail), continuing past the hillside on the right. Follow the Wonderland/Old Trail for 1.5 miles farther as it slowly curves to the northeast, to the point where it ends in a sandy wash. See map page 60.

The Atom Smashers

This area lies about 3 miles (4.8 km) from Key's Corner Parking area. Hike along the Wonderland Trail to where it ends in a sandy wash. Straight ahead (east by northeast) a group of angular-shaped boulders and formations can be seen. Although the main wash now heads south, follow a narrow streambed east until you reach an open basin. The main Atom Smashers area lies directly ahead. See map and approach information page 63.

The Ivory Tower

The large (main) formations on the hillside are referred to as the Timbuktu Towers. The largest formation has many routes on the west and south faces. The large, leaning pillar high on the north side of the Timbuktu Towers is the Ivory Tower. The following four routes lie on its overhanging north face. See map page 63.

13 *The Powers That Be*   5.13a ★★★   This route has 5 bolts and is near the left edge of the face.

14 *Chain of Addiction*   5.13c ★★★   Climb the center of the face past 9 bolts.

15 *Ocean of Doubt*   5.13b/c ★★★   This route is just right of Chain of Addiction.

16 *La Machine*   5.13d ★★★   This route is near the right edge and has 6 bolts.

Atom Smasher Boulders

These boulders lie about 125 yards south-southeast and down the hill from the main Timbuktu Towers formation. The boulders are generally about fifty feet high. Many face climbs ranging from 5.9 to 5.12a are found on the sharp arêtes. Map page 63.

The Super Dome

From the point where the Wonderland/Old Trail ends in a sandy wash, follow the sandy wash south for a few hundred yards to where it curves to the east. (See pages 60 and 63.) Continue to follow the main wash as it winds roughly eastward until you reach a open area with several large ponds of water. This is Willow Hole. Willow Hole serves as a year-round watering area for desert wildlife, including endangered bighorn sheep. Please keep human impact to a minimum. From Willow Hole proper, walk east along Rattlesnake Canyon about 200 yards. A narrow canyon heading north can be seen from here. Follow talus up this canyon to the base of the obvious and beautiful Super Dome. See map page 63.

(routes listed on topo on next page)

The Super Block

This formation lies immediately to the right of The Super Dome. To approach the routes, start at the base of Chief Crazy Horse. "Third class" (5.6) up the slab to the right (you actually can use this to avoid the first pitch of Chief Crazy Horse) until a bolt anchor is reached. Stem out right and traverse around to the south face of the rock. The following routes lie on the south face. See map page 63.

(routes listed on topo on next page)

The Super Dome
(see previous page for directions)

17 **Warpath** 5.12c ★★★
18 **The Last Unicorn** 5.11a R ★★★

The Super Block
(see previous page for directions)

19 **Sideburn** 5.12a ★   Climb over the roof and continue up the southwest arête. This is the left-most route on the formation.

20 **Hydra** 5.13c ★★★   This bolt-protected route leads up to the crest of the "wave-like" face to the right of Sideburn.

21 **Lion's Share** 5.10b ★★   This route climbs the arête to the right of Hydra.

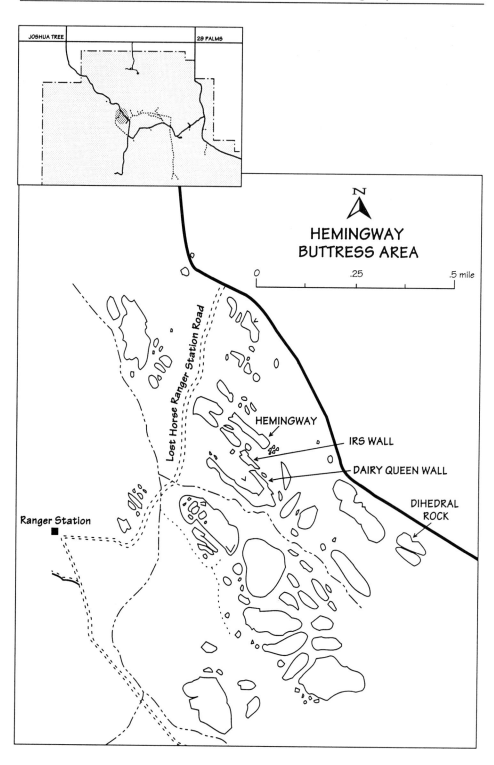

Hemingway Buttress Area

The routes and crags described in this section lie to the south of the junction of Quail Springs Road and the Ranger Station Road, and are all approached from Quail Springs Road. The Ranger Station Road lies approximately 8 miles from the monument entrance and 1.6 miles from Hidden Valley Campground (heading toward the town of Joshua Tree). Crags and routes approached directly from the Ranger Station Road are described in the immediately preceding section. Parking for all of these routes is at the Hemingway Parking area. This well-defined parking area is located 0.2 mile south of the Quail Springs-Ranger Station Road junction on the west side of the road. Trail markers indicate the approach trails to all of these crags. Please use only the marked trails to reduce your impact on the desert landscape. See map page 66.

Hemingway Buttress East Face

This long formation lies about 200 yards directly west of the Hemingway Parking area. The parking area is located approximately 0.2 mile south of the Quail Springs-Ranger Station Road junction. The formation has many fine crack climbs on the east face (facing the road). From the parking area follow the marked trail straight west to the base of the cliff (near the vicinity of White Lightning). Other routes may be accessed by traversing the base of the cliff. Map page 66.

Descents: There are many descent routes off Hemingway Buttress, largely dependent upon which route you have climbed. A bolted rappel anchor is located just right of the top of White Lightning; two ropes are required. Down-climbs are possible from any route. Consult the topos for exact locations of descent routes.

22 *Overseer* 5.9 ★★ Climb shallow corner, then go right over the roof (easier than it looks). Pro: thin to 2 inches.

22a *Direct Start* 5.10a ★ Recommended start, up thin cracks; pro a little tricky. Pro: Thin.

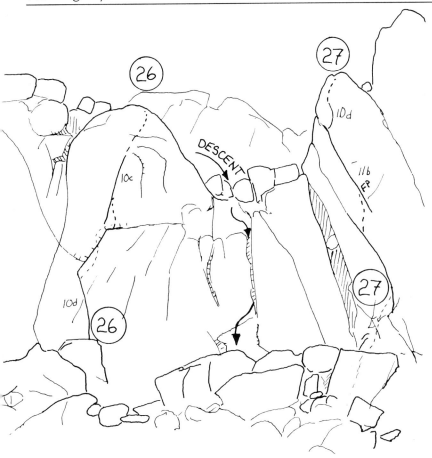

23   *White Lightning*   5.7 ★ Obvious straight-in crack. Pro: 1 to 3 inches.

24   *Poodles Are People Too*   5.10b ★★ This is the very thin crack just right of White Lightning; face climbing with crack protection. Pro: many thin to 1.5 inches.

25   *Prepackaged* 5.10a ★★ Take diagonal thin crack which widens over bulge. Pro: To 2.5 inches.

26   *The Importance Of Being Ernest* 5.10d R ★ Crux down low leads over roof to very shallow cracks near the top; some dubious fixed copperheads. Pro: Very thin to 2 inches.

27   *Scary Poodles* 5.11b ★★   Start up lower crack, switch over to upper crack. Continue past a fixed pin, then up "arch" at top. Pro: Thin to 1 inch.

28   *Head Over Heals*   5.10a ★★ This route lies about 150 feet right of Scary Poodles, on the right-hand arête/corner of the main Hemingway Buttress formation. Climb up a dihedral, traverse left past a bolt and follow a hand crack around the corner to the top. Pro: 1 bolt, gear to 2.5 inches.

The IRS Wall

This formation lies about 75 yards behind and to the left (southwest) of Hemingway Buttress. To approach the rock, follow the marked trail from the Hemingway Parking area for about 120 yards. At this point the trail splits; take the left fork, which leads toward the IRS and Dairy Queen Walls. See map page 66.

29 *Alf's Arête*   5.11a ★★★ This route lies on the extreme left (southeast) corner of the IRS Wall. Great bolted face climbing up the arête. Pro: 7 bolts.

30 *Tax Man*   5.10a ★★★ This is the straight-in thin crack near the right-hand side of the IRS Wall (50 yards right of Alf's Arête). It is clearly visible from the road and is about 100 feet in height. Descend to the right (north) and down a narrow chimney that separates The IRS Wall from The Copenhagen Wall. Pro: thin to 2.5 inches.

Dairy Queen Wall

This formation lies to the left (south) of the IRS Wall and about 150 yards southwest of Hemingway Buttress. Its right section is very knobby and has several cracks of varying widths. These routes are generally good moderate routes, although protection may be tricky. For this reason they are often top-roped. See map page 66.

31 *Scrumdillyishus* 5.7 ★
32 *Frosty Cone* 5.7 ★★
33 *Chili Dog* 5.10a ★ Pro: Small wires to 2 inches.
34 *Mr. Misty Kiss* 5.7 ★★
35 *Double Decker* 5.6 ★

Dihedral Rock

This formation lies on the west side of the Quail Springs Road, about 1.2 mile from Hidden Valley Campground, and 0.8 mile south of the junction of Ranger Station Road and Quail Springs Road. The large, left-facing dihedral on its left side can be seen easily from the road. See map page 66.

36 ***Coarse and Buggy*** 5.11a ★★★ This routes goes up the obvious left-facing dihedral. Pro: many thin to 2 inches.

37 ***Sow Sickle*** 5.11d ★★ This route lies on the right side of the east face, about 50 feet right of Coarse and Buggy, face climbing up to a thin crack. Pro: Bolts, fixed pins and small to medium nuts.

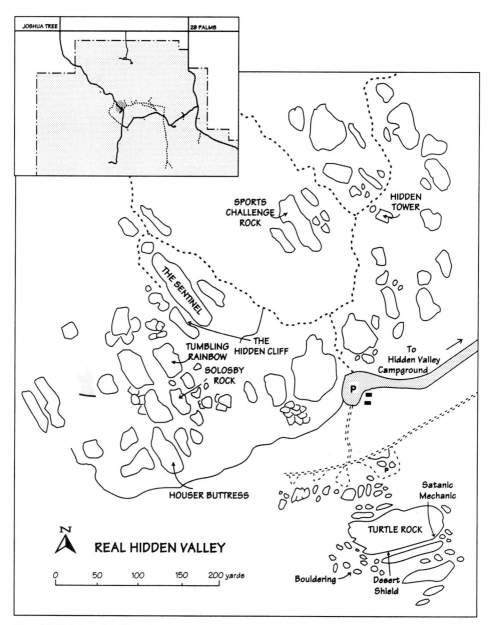

Real Hidden Valley Area

Just before the Hidden Valley Campground is a road that heads southwest from the Quail Springs Road. This road leads to the Real Hidden Valley. At the end of the paved section of the Real Hidden Valley Road is a parking area. The entrance to the Real Hidden Valley is to the north: a sign and trail marker make this obvious. A Nature Trail makes a loop circuit of Real Hidden Valley. Reference is made to this trail in describing the locations of various formations.

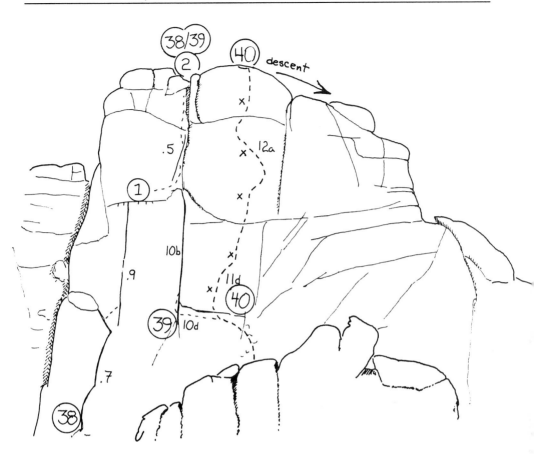

Sports Challenge Rock

This excellent formation lies roughly in the central part of the Real Hidden Valley, and is one of the best (and most popular) rock formations in this area. Most routes on Sports Challenge Rock are easily (and commonly) top-roped. Nevertheless, almost all the routes may be led. To get to the formation, follow the nature trail out of the parking area into Real Hidden Valley. From here, the west face of Sports Challenge Rock will be seen about 100 yards to the northeast. See map page 72.

Descent: Fourth-class climbing down the south shoulder (this is the easiest way to the top).

West Face

The west face sports mostly vertical crack and face routes on solid dark-brown rock. A good assortment of thin to medium protection is helpful in protecting most of these climbs.

    38   *Sphincter Quits* 5.9 ★★ Pro: To 2 inches.
    39   *What's It To You* 5.10d ★★ Use the first bolt of Rap Bolters Are Weak to protect the initial traverse. Pro: Thin to 1.5 inches.
    40   *Rap Bolters Are Weak* 5.12a ★★ Pro: 4 bolts, to 3 inches for anchors.

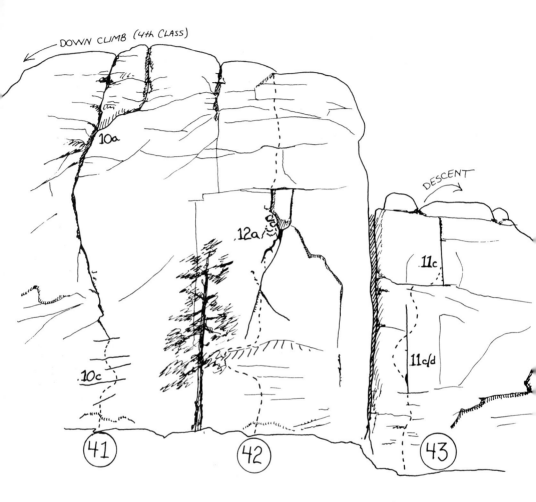

Sports Challenge Rock East Face

The east face is continuously overhanging and has many excellent crack and face climbs. Excellent boulder problems and traverse are located on the face just below Leave It To Beaver. See map page 72.

41 *Clean and Jerk* 5.10c ★★★ The start is the crux; a good spotter is helpful to prevent a ground fall until the crack is reached. Pro: To 3 inches.

42 *Leave it to Beaver* 5.12a ★★★ Most people top-rope this route, although reasonable natural protection is available. An extension runner (or rope) of about 25 feet is needed for a top rope. Pro: To 4 inches.

43 *Cool but Concerned* 5.11d ★★ This route starts about 5 feet right of the obvious off-width crack 25 feet right of Leave It To Beaver. Follow a thin seam/crack to a horizontal; traverse right to a crack leading to the top. Pro: Many small to 1.5 inches.

Hidden Tower

This small tower is to the east of Sports Challenge Rock and just east of the Nature Trail. To get to the formation, follow the Nature Trail out of the parking area into Real Hidden Valley. From here, take the right-hand fork in the trail (heading east). Continue on the trail over a wooden bridge; a short distance farther, the trail heads straight north and the formation lies directly to your east. Hike to the left (north) of the formation to get to the east face routes. The formation also can be reached easily from Quail Springs Road by walking southwest from a point approximately 0.2 mile north of the Hidden Valley Campground entrance. See map page 72.

44 *Sail Away* 5.8- ★★★ This is the fine right-hand crack of two cracks on the northeast face. Pro: To 2 inches.

Kevin Powell

Mike Waugh on *Chameleon* 5.12b

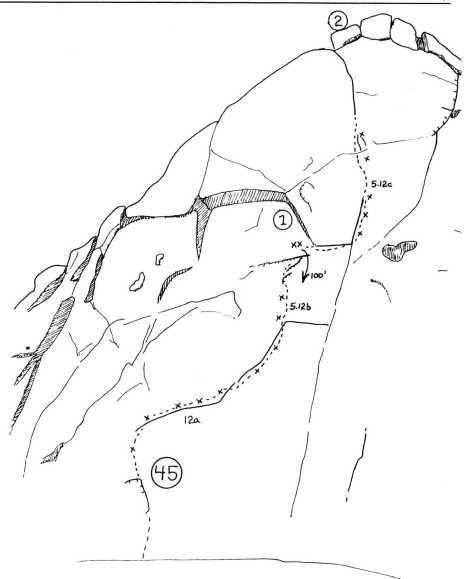

The Sentinel

This large formation lies on the west side of the Real Hidden Valley and sports two large faces. To get to the formation, follow the nature trail out of the parking area into Real Hidden Valley. From here, take the left-hand fork of the Nature Trail (northwest). The east face is found about fifty yards after the fork, on the left (western) side of the Nature Trail. The west face is hidden; it lies in a narrow canyon. The easiest approach is to follow the Nature Trail just past the east face, then cut off to the left (west) over a few small boulders. The west face is reached via a well-used trail running back south into the canyon. It has many fine routes and is approximately 200 feet high at its tallest point. See map page 72.

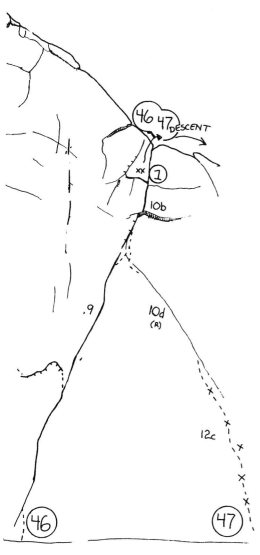

West Face

45 **Some Like It Hot** 5.12c ★★★ The first pitch is 5.12b. Pro: 8 bolts. The second pitch is 5.12c. Pro: To 3 inches; 4 bolts. Rap from end of first pitch requires second rope.

46 **Illusion Dweller** (aka Candy-Colored Tangerine Flake Streamlined Baby) 5.10b ★★★ Pro: several thin to 3 inches. 2 ropes needed to rap from bolt anchor, easy walk off up and to the right.

47 **The Chameleon** 5.12b R ★★ A bit runout above the bolts, pro hard to get in upper crack. Pro: 5 bolts, nuts to 3 inches.

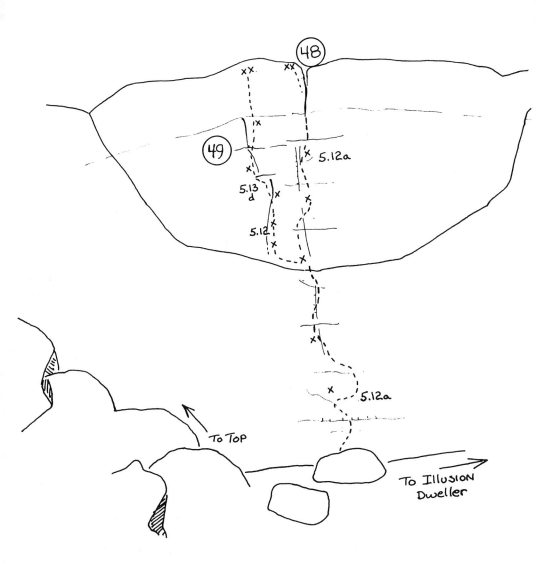

The Hidden Cliff

This cliff lies opposite the west face of the Sentinel, about 75 feet further south from The Chameleon, in a narrow canyon/gully area. It is a very nice, slightly overhanging face that is in the shade almost all day. This is a good choice for hot days. Routes can easily be top-roped from bolt anchors on top. See map page 72.

48 *Bikini Whale* 5.12b ★★ Climbs knobs and horizontal bands straight up. Stick clip of first bolt may be desirable. Pro: 5 bolts.

49 *G String* 5.13d ★★ Climb Bikini Whale to a horizontal crack then go left a short distance, then up a thin flake/corner and face. Pro: 8 bolts.

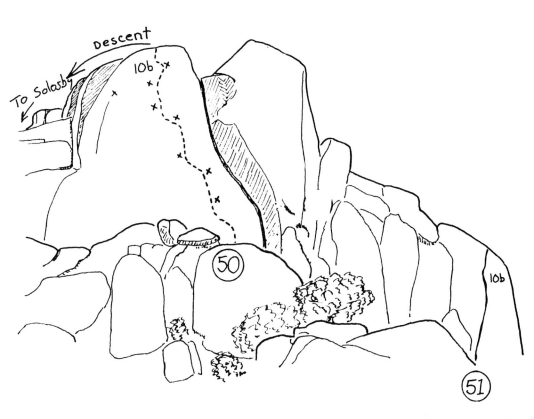

Tumbling Rainbow Formation

This is the highest point in the Real Hidden Valley. To get to the formation, follow the nature trail out of the parking area into Real Hidden Valley; it is located about 175 yards to the west. Take the left-hand fork of the Nature Trail for about 20 yards, then head west along a small wash until boulder-hopping leads to the base.

50 ***Run for Your Life*** 5.10b ★★★ A little run-out to first bolt. Bring medium nuts for anchors on top. Descend to the left down past the Solosby Face. Pro: 6 bolts.

51 ***Fisticuffs*** 5.10b ★ Pro: To 4 inches.

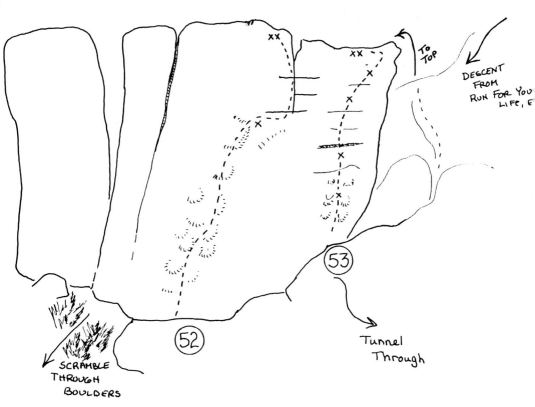

Solosby Face

This overhanging, knobby, orange-colored face lies to the left (south) of the Tumbling Rainbow Formation and behind a series of blocks that face the trail. The descent from Tumbling Rainbow leads past this face. To reach it from below, follow the nature trail out of the parking area into Real Hidden Valley. Take the left-hand fork of the Nature Trail for about 20 yards, then head west along a small wash until boulder-hopping leads to a scramble up between huge blocks to the left of the Tumbling Rainbow Face. See map page 72.

52 *Latin Swing* 5.11c ★ This route ascends the center of the face before traversing right to a thin crack. Best top-roped. Pro: Thin to 2 inches, 1 bolt.

53 *Bebop Tango* 5.11a/b ★★ Climb buckets and holds on the right side of the face. Pro: 4 bolts.

Turtle Rock

This large formation lies 150 yards south of the main parking area for the Real Hidden Valley. Many routes have been established on the south and east faces. The area to the southwest of Turtle Rock sports some of the best bouldering in Joshua Tree. Many fine (and high off-the-deck) problems are found here. This is the site of the famous So High Boulder. For bouldering information see the comprehensive guide (*Joshua Tree Rock Climbing Guide, Second Edition*), or *Joshua Tree Bouldering Guide* by Mari Gingery.

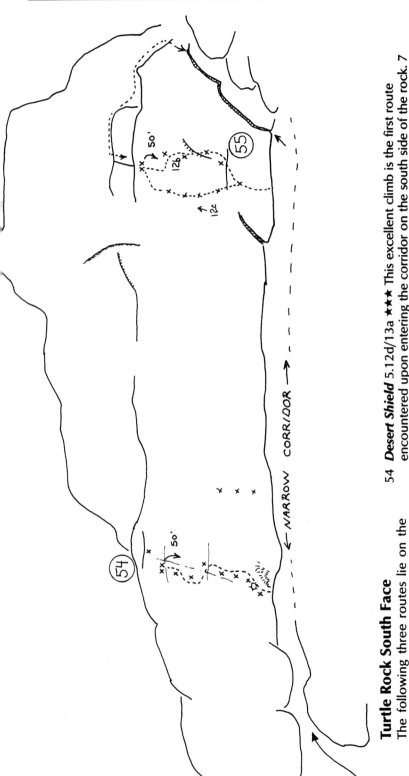

Turtle Rock South Face

The following three routes lie on the western end of the south face in a small corridor formed by rocks to the south. They are best approached by walking around the western end of the rock and entering the corridor near at its west end. See map page 72.

54 **Desert Shield** 5.12d/13a ★★★ This excellent climb is the first route encountered upon entering the corridor on the south side of the rock. 7 bolts lead to cold-shut hooks; one rope reaches on lowering. Setting up a top-rope requires a belay and/or medium to 3-inch pro and a second rope.

55 **Satanic Mechanic** 5.12b ★★★ This fine sport route climbs up and right to a crack/roof, then heads out left and up to hook anchors. One rope lowers. A belay may be necessary to set up a top-rope off the fixed biners.

Houser Buttress

A dirt trail leads west along the outside perimeter of the Real Hidden Valley from the western end of the Real Hidden Valley parking area. This ridge of rocks and buttresses can be seen easily from the parking\picnic area near the northwestern corner of Turtle Rock. A prominent buttress of rock (Houser Buttress) is approximately 225 yards to the west. See map page 72.

   56 *Loose Lady* 5.9+ ★★★ Pro: Bolts, 2-bolt anchor/rap.
   57 *Puss n' Boots* 5.11c ★ Pro: Bolts, 2-bolt anchor/rap.

Hidden Valley Campground

This campground is the true center of the Joshua Tree scene. Most climbers camp here, although a 14-day limit can be enforced. The rocks surrounding the campground offer many good to excellent routes. There is good bouldering throughout the campground area. These are described in the comprehensive guide (*Joshua Tree Rock Climbing Guide, Second Edition*), and *Joshua Tree Bouldering Guide* by Mari Gingery.

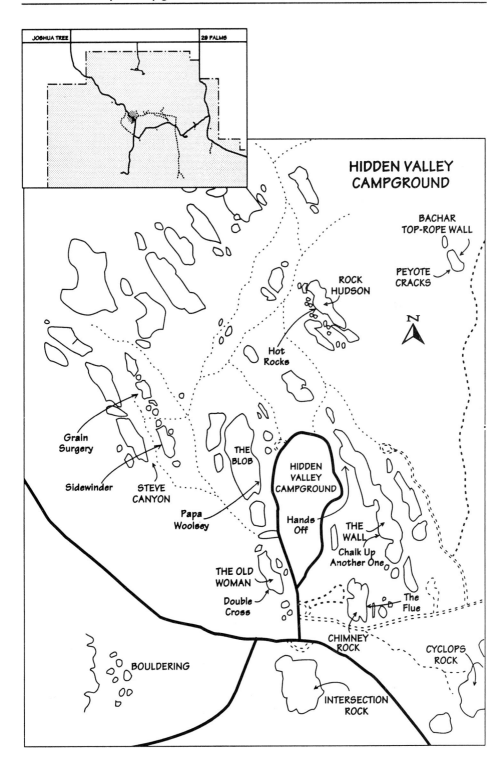

HIDDEN VALLEY
CAMPGROUND

JOSHUA TREE   29 PALMS

BACHAR
TOP-ROPE WALL

PEYOTE
CRACKS

ROCK
HUDSON

Hot
Rocks

N

Grain
Surgery

THE
BLOB

HIDDEN
VALLEY
CAMPGROUND

Sidewinder   STEVE
CANYON

Papa
Woolsey

Hands
Off

THE
WALL

Chalk Up
Another One

THE OLD
WOMAN

Double
Cross

The
Flue

CHIMNEY
ROCK

CYCLOPS
ROCK

BOULDERING

INTERSECTION
ROCK

Intersection Rock

This formation lies just south of the main entrance to, and across Quail Springs Road from, Hidden Valley Campground.

Descent: The most popular descent is via two 75-foot rappels from the top of Mike's Books. A 90-foot rappel can be done from atop North Overhang to the large ledge. Advanced climbers often downclimb Upper Right Ski Track (5.3) to the Large Ledge. Other (Class 5) downclimbs are possible. See map page 83.

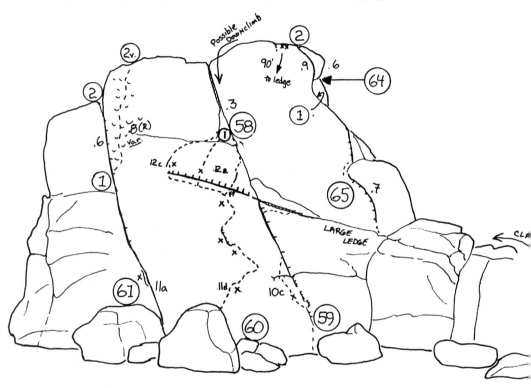

North Face (facing road)
58 *Upper Right Ski Track* 5.3
59 *Lower Right Ski Track* 5.10c ★
60 *Trapeze* 5.11d ★
61 *Left Ski Track* 5.11a ★★ Pro: 1 bolt, several medium, up to 4 inches.

South Face
62 *Mike's Books* 5.6 ★ This route climbs an obvious and large right-facing dihedral system on the southern part of the rock. Start to the left and below the dihedral; face climb up and right of the start of the corner. (Variation: climb a short thin hand crack in a small flake/corner straight up to the dihedral [5.8+]). Climb the dihedral to a large ledge. Above, climb another dihedral which leads to face climbing past a bolt to rappel anchors. Rap the route (two 75-foot rappels). Pro: To 3 inches.

West Face

63 **The Flake** 5.8 ★ This route starts on the West Face around the corner from the start of North Overhang, etc. Starts 40 feet right of Overhang Bypass. Climb a chimney for 40 feet to a left-facing flake system that ends high on the face; above 2 bolts protect face climbing (5.8) to the top.

64 **Overhang Bypass** 5.7 ★★ Climb shallow crack systems directly up to a small, cave-like overhang; climb directly up or to the left to reach a large sloping belay ledge beneath the large overhang near the summit (same belay ledge as for North Overhang). An exciting traverse left leads to face climbing past 1 bolt to the top.

65 **North Overhang** 5.9 ★★ This route starts off the ledge that leads up to Upper Ski Track. Climb a flake/crack to a ledge, just below the summit overhang. Climb out and left around the overhang, along a crack to the top.

Kevin Powell

Tom Gilje and Mari Gingery on *Street Sweeper,* 5.11+, Echo Rock

The Old Woman – East Face

This is the first formation on the left (west) as you enter the campground.

Descent: Most climbers rappel (80 feet) from one of three anchors (atop Double Cross or Bearded Cabbage, or at the bottom of Geronimo); see topos. See map page 83.

66 *Toe Jam* 5.7 ★ Pro: To 2.5 inches.
67 *Bearded Cabbage* 5.10c ★ Pro: To 3 inches; 1 bolt.
68 *Spider Line* 5.11c ★★ Pro: Thin to 2.5 inches.
69 *Geronimo* 5.7 ★★

The Old Woman – West Face

70 *Dogleg* 5.8 ★ Pro: To 2.5 inches.
71 *Double Cross* 5.7+ ★★ Pro: To 3 inches.
72 *Orphan* 5.9 ★★ Pro: To 3 inches.

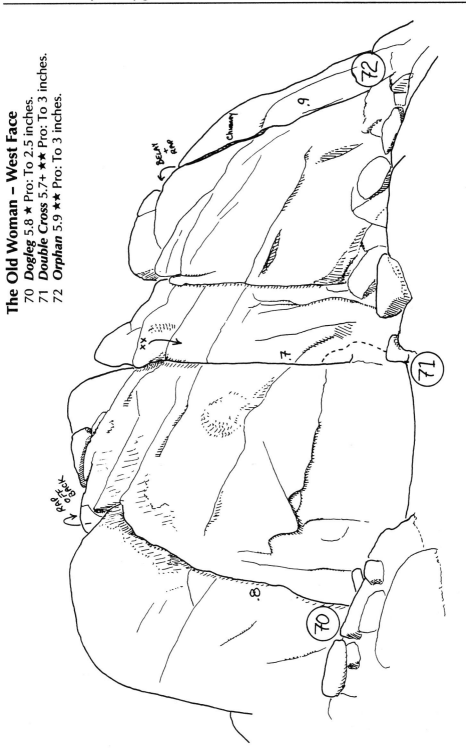

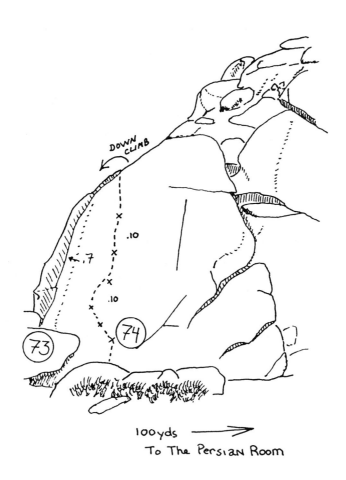

DOWN CLIMB

.10

.7

.10

73

74

100 yds

To The Persian Room

The Blob – East Face

This aptly-named formation lies on the left (west) side of the campground, near its north end.

Descent: Downclimb down chimney and blocks (5.0); See topo. Map page 83.

73 *Buissonier* 5.7 ★ Pro: thin to 2 inches.
74 *Papa Woolsey* 5.10b ★ Pro: bolts; bring medium pro for anchors.

The Wall

This formation is a very long, somewhat discontinuous wall located directly east of both The Blob and The Old Woman. Its north end starts just south of Outhouse Rock and extends south to a point just east of Chimney Rock. See map page 83.

The Wall – North End

Directly east of the vertical east face of The Blob, and just south of Outhouse Rock is the northern end of The Wall. The straight-in crack on the right is Hands Off.

75 *Hands Off* 5.8 ★ The obvious straight-in crack mentioned above. Pro: thin to 2 inches.

The Wall – South End

The southern end of The Wall lies about 40 yards northeast of Chimney Rock and faces west toward the campground. It is easily seen from the bulletin board area, and is characterized as a smooth face split by a chimney system. The following climbs lie on the section of face just right of the chimney system.

76 *Chalk Up Another One* 5.9+ ★★ Start 25 feet right of the obvious chimney in the middle of the formation, climb up and left past 5 bolts to easier ground; a sixth bolt protects entry to a flared crack leading to the top. Pro: 6 bolts, gear to 2.5 inches.

77 *Pumping Ego* 5.10b Start about 12 feet right of Chalk Up Another One (35 feet right of the obvious chimney) climb up past 2 bolts then head up and right past 2 more bolts. Pro: 4 bolts, nuts for anchor.

Chimney Rock – West Face

This rock is located at the east side of the campground, just east of where the dirt road to Echo Cove and Barker Dam heads off the paved loop road.

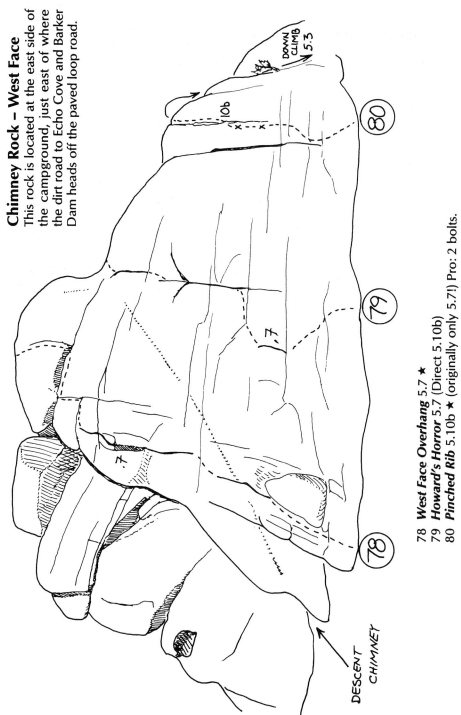

78 *West Face Overhang* 5.7 ★
79 *Howard's Horror* 5.7 (Direct 5.10b)
80 *Pinched Rib* 5.10b ★ (originally only 5.7!) Pro: 2 bolts.

Chimney Rock – East Face

81   *The Flue* 5.8 ★ This route lies left of the middle of the east side of Chimney Rock. Face climb up horizontals to reach an obvious right-diagonalling crack system that ends in a cave. Descend down the chimney/gully on the west face. Pro: To 3 inches.

Cyclops Rock

This formation lies outside Hidden Valley Campground, about 300 yards east of the entrance.

Cyclops Rock – Northwest Face

82   *Surface Tension* 5.10d ★ Start about 20 feet left of the start of the Eye, by jumping up to a "hole"; 4 bolts protect face climbing up and left. Scary to the first bolt. Pro: 4 bolts, nuts to 2.5 inches (anchors).

83   *The Eye* 5.3 R ★★ The Eye ascends the back of the obvious and large central recess on the West face of Cyclops Rock. The route tops out at the "Eye." Pro: To 3 inches.

84   *Leader's Fright* 5.8 R ★ Class 3 up a steep gully (5.0) 70 feet to the right of the start of the Eye to a large ledge. Climb the crack system which starts near the right end of ledge. Pro: To 2 inches.

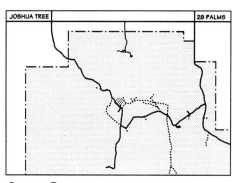

The Outback

This area covers territory starting northwest of Hidden Valley Campground and continuing east in an arc to just west of the Echo Rock/Echo Cove area.

Steve Canyon

This group of rocks lies 200 yards northwest of the gap between The Old Woman and the Blob. They can be approached easily from either the campground or from pullouts along Quail Springs Road located about a quarter-mile northwest of the campground. The formations form a canyon that runs in a north/south direction. Routes lie both within the canyon as well as on the east and west faces "outside" the canyon. See map page 83.

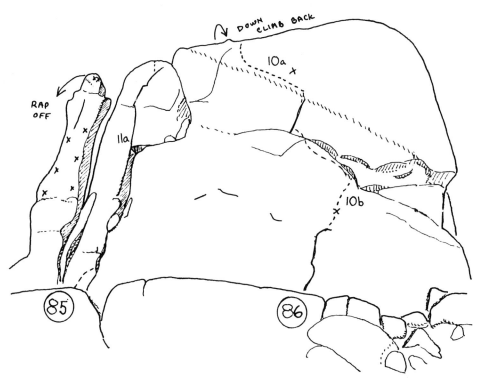

Steve Canyon – Lower East Side (West Face)

85 *Jumping Jack Crack* 5.11a ★★ Pro: To 2 inches.
86 *Sidewinder* 5.10b ★★★ Pro: Medium to 2.5 inches.

Steve Canyon – Upper East Side (West Face)

This formation lies to the left and up the canyon from The previous climbs. A large chimney system splits this upper face.

Descent: Downclimb to the left (facing cliff), down to very large wedged boulder then under it into gully (5.0).

87 *Grain Surgery* 5.10b R ★★ This is the left-most route on the face. Climb a shallow crack to a bolt to a horizontal; above 1 more bolt protects face climbing to the top. Pro: Cams to 2 inches.

88 *The Decompensator of Lhasa* 5.10d ★★ Start 15 feet right of the chimney (see above), up a left-curving shallow crack to horizontals. Above 4 bolts protect face climbing up, then right on the arête. Pro: Several 0.5 to 2 inches.

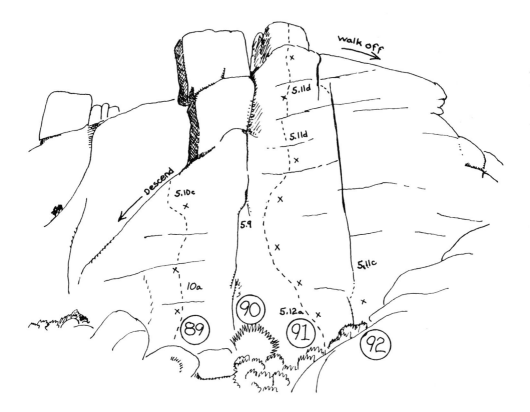

Rock Hudson

Rock Hudson is located about 150 yards north of Outhouse Rock. See map page 83.

89 *Absolute Zero* 5.10c

90 *Looney Tunes* 5.9 ★

91 *Stand and Deliver* 5.12a ★★ Pro: 8 bolts, 0.5 to 1.5-inch camming units for horizontals.

92 *Hot Rocks* 5.11c ★★★ Pro: Several thin to 3 inches.

Peyote Cracks

This small but oft-climbed formation is about 250 yards northeast of Rock Hudson; roughly halfway between Hidden Valley Campground and Echo Cove. Its west face is less vertical and has three prominent cracks. The east face is overhanging and contains a number of excellent and difficult routes. The formation is an easy walk from Hidden Valley Campground. A small parking area near Echo Cove Rocks also provides good access. See map page 83.

Peyote Cracks – West Face

The west face has three obvious cracks (Left, Middle and Right Peyote Cracks).

93 *Left Peyote Crack* 5.10 ★ Pro: To 2 inches.
94 *Middle Peyote Crack* 5.9 ★ Pro: To 2 inches.
95 *Right Peyote Crack* 5.8 ★ Pro: To 2.5 inches.

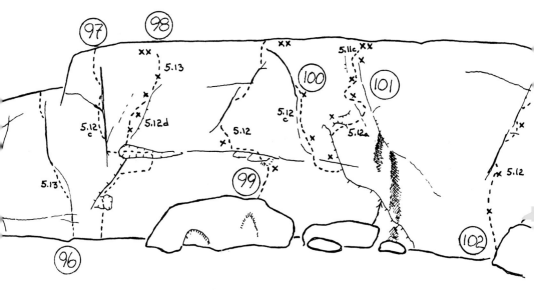

Peyote Cracks – East Face (aka Bachar Top-Rope Wall)

This overhanging face contains many difficult and excellent routes. Many of these routes were top-rope problems that have since been lead; in some cases, bolts have been added to protect these leads. Most of these routes are good sport climbs.

96 *The Moonbeam Crack* 5.13a ★ This route has been led, but most prefer a top-rope. Pro: From 0.25 to 2 inches.
97 *Baby Apes* 5.12c ★★ Pro: Thin to 2 inches. Most will top-rope.
98 *Rastafarian* 5.13b Pro: Thin to 2 inches, 4 bolts.
99 *The Watusi* 5.12c ★ Pro: To 2 inches, 3 bolts.
100 *Dial Africa* 5.12c ★★ Pro: Very thin to 2 inches, 4 bolts (poorly located).
101 *Apartheid* 5.12a ★★ Pro: 4 bolts, 1.5 inch cam optional.
102 *Buffalo Soldier* 5.12b ★ Pro: To 2 inches, 4 bolts.

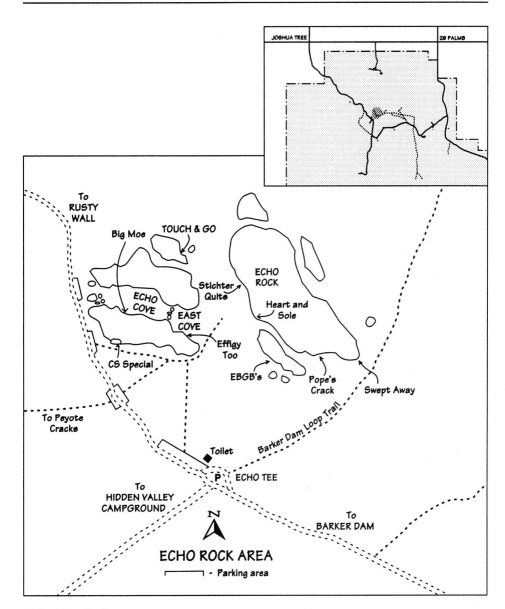

ECHO ROCK AREA

⌐‾‾‾‾¬ - Parking area

Echo Rock Area

This area lies about 0.7 mile to the northeast of Hidden Valley Campground. The dirt road leading to Echo Rock begins just south of Chimney Rock. A large parking area marks the spot where the road "tees" (Echo Tee). The road is called Big Horn Pass Road. The road to the northwest leads to Keys Ranch, an old ranch site that is off-limits to all but guided tours. If you head right (east) from Echo Tee, you'll pass parking areas for the Comic Book Area, Barker Dam and Wonderland of Rocks, and eventually get back to the main, paved monument road (Queen Valley Road). Please use established trails to avoid damaging the native vegetation.

Rusty Wall

From Echo Cove (.25 mile north of Echo Tee), follow the dirt road (may be closed) for about 0.75 mile to a gate/fence for Keys Ranch. A short hike west (of about 400 yards) leads to the base of this orange-tinted, overhanging wall. Two cracks are located on the wall.

   103 *Wangerbanger* 5.11c ★★★ This is the left crack.

   104 *O'Kelley's Crack* 5.10c ★★★ This is the right crack. The start is 5.11.

Echo Cove

This little "cove" lies about 0.25 mile northwest of Echo Tee, on the right (east) side of the road. Routes are described in sequence as they lie on each wall of the cove. Right and left are used in reference to how you would view the walls if you were facing east into the cove.

Descent: Routes 106 to 109 down the gully/chimney just left of R.A.F. (5.0).

Peter Croft on *O'Kelley's Crack*, 5.10c

Echo Cove – Left (North) Side

105 *Fun Stuff* 5.8 This route climbs the dark buttress on the left end of the wall directly to a 2-bolt anchor/rappel. Pro: To 2 inches.

106 *The Sound of One Shoe Tapping* 5.8 This 3-bolt route lies on the left side of the light-colored buttress 40 feet right of Fun Stuff.

107 *W.A.C.* 5.8 This is a 2-bolt route on the right side of the light-colored buttress, 40 feet right of Fun Stuff.

108 *Pepason* 5.9+ A 3-bolt climb on a small buttress 30 feet right W.A.C.

109 *R.A.F.* 5.9 ★ A 3-bolt climb on the mottled face, 100 feet right of Fun Stuff, and just right of a low-angle, chimney/gully (descent route).

Echo Cove – Right (South) Side

The following routes lie on the steep right-hand end of the south (right) side of Echo Cove, almost directly opposite Fun Stuff/W.A.C.

110 *Big Moe* 5.11a R/X ★★★ This route lies about 35 feet left of a black water streak, to the left of a large oak bush/tree. A difficult move above a scoop leads past horizontal cracks and a fun finish. Usually top-roped (bolts on top).

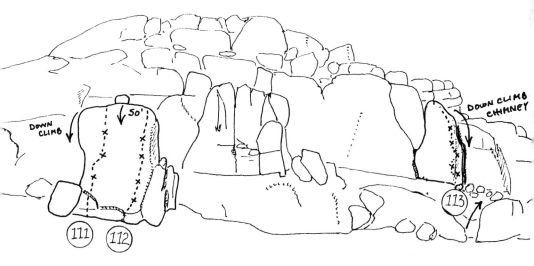

Echo Cove Rocks – South Face

The Echo Cove Rocks form the cove itself, and the outer faces of these rocks contain many fine routes. The south face faces the Big Horn Pass Road.

111 *R.M.L.* 5.8 ★★

112 *C.S. Special* 5.10b ★★ The start may be quite hard for shorter people.

113 *Out on a Limb* 5.10b ★★ Pro: 5 bolts. The start may be more difficult if you're under 5'11" or so.

East Cove Rocks

This small cove actually is a continuation of Echo Cove itself; a pile of boulders separates the two areas. A trail connects the two. It lies about 75 yards right (east) of C.S. Special, just around the corner from Out On A Limb. See map page 95.

East Cove – Left Side

The east side of this small "cove" of rock is steep brown rock. Near the right side of the face a hand crack starts about 15 feet off the ground; this crack is Effigy Too. The easiest descent is down a chimney/gully directly behind the face. The other side of the chimney is formed by the large boulder containing Out On A Limb. You end up at the start of that route. See topo page 97.

114 *Halfway to Paradise* 5.10a R ★★ Start this route about 20 feet left of Effigy Too, climb up and left to a small sloping ledge, continue up past a bolt, then back right following easier climbing past many horizontal cracks. Pro: Many cams to 2 inches, 1 bolt.

115 *Effigy Too* 5.10a/b ★★ Several difficult moves up and left give access to the bottom of the obvious hand crack near the right-hand end of the face. Pro: Thin to 2 inches.

East Cove – Right Side

This wall directly faces Effigy Too, etc. (faces southwest).

116 *Solo Dog* 5.11b ★★ Near the right end of the face, face climb up a very thin crack to a horizontal break, then up past 3 bolts. Pro: Very thin to 1 inch, 3 bolts.

Echo Cove Formations – East Side

An east-facing part of the Echo Cove Rock is about 110 yards to the right of East Cove, and roughly opposite the northwestern end of Echo Rock. The excellent-looking left-facing corner is Touch and Go. See map page 95.

117 *Touch and Go* 5.9 ★★★

Echo Rock

This rock lies nearly straight ahead (northeast) of the parking area at Echo Tee. The North (left) End is directly across from the east side of the Echo Cove formation. The South (right) End is best reached via an excellent trail (a continuation of an old road) that starts at the Echo Tee parking lot. This trail (Barker Dam Loop Trail) also provides easy access to the Candy Bar Area. Climber trail markers have been placed to reduce the proliferation of "braided" trails through this area. Please reduce your impact on the desert by following these marked paths. Also, a toilet is located at the Echo Tee parking area. If you are climbing anywhere in the vicinity, please use this facility rather than leaving your waste in the desert. See map page 95.

Echo Rock – North End, West Face

The west face of Echo Rock, due to its good rock and moderate angle, is ideally suited to face climbing. Theoretically, face climbs can be done almost anywhere, and the following list of routes clearly demonstrates this point. The addition of new bolted climbs only detracts from the existing routes. There are many excellent faces awaiting first ascents elsewhere in the monument; new route attention should be directed to those projects.

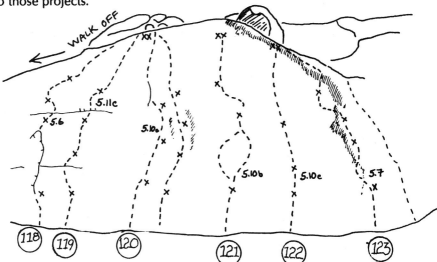

118 *Double Dip* 5.6 ★
119 *Battle of the Bulge* 5.11c/d ★
120 *Try Again* 5.10c ★
121 *Gone in 60 Seconds* 5.10a R ★
122 *Cherry Bomb* 5.10c ★
123 *Stichter Quits* 5.7 ★★

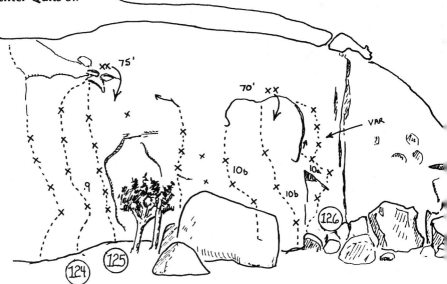

124 *Stick to What* 5.9 ★★
125 *Forbidden Paradise* 5.10b ★★★
126 *Heart and Sole* 5.10a ★★★

EBGB Area

A large block (the EBGB's Block) sits high on a pile of rocks to the right and west of the West Face of Echo Rock. A narrow corridor runs between the block and Echo Rock. The large block has several high-angled face routes on it. Descend off the block down a chimney on the back (east) side. See map page 95.

127 ***EBGB's*** 5.10d ★★★ This route starts near the southwest corner of the EBGB's Block. A difficult move up leads to an easy traverse out onto the west face; continue up to the top. A *little* run-out past last bolt. Pro: 5 bolts.

Kevin Powell

Mari Gingery on *Father Figure*, 5.12d

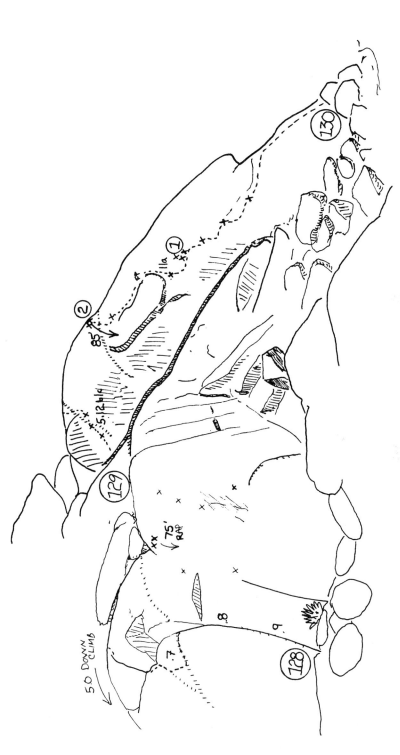

Echo Rock – South End

Descent from Pope's Crack, etc. is either by walking off to the left, down a gully/chimney and through boulders, or rappel from 2 bolts down and to the right. Descent for Sole Fusion and Swept Away is via 85 foot rappel from the top of the second pitch of Swept Away.

128 **Pope's Crack** 5.9 ★★ Pro: To 2.5 inches.
129 **Sole Fusion** 5.12a ★★ Pro: 3 bolts, nuts for anchors.
130 **Swept Away** 5.11a ★★★ Start at the base of the buttress, then traverse out left below roof. Pro: Thin to 1 inch, 5 bolts, fixed pin.

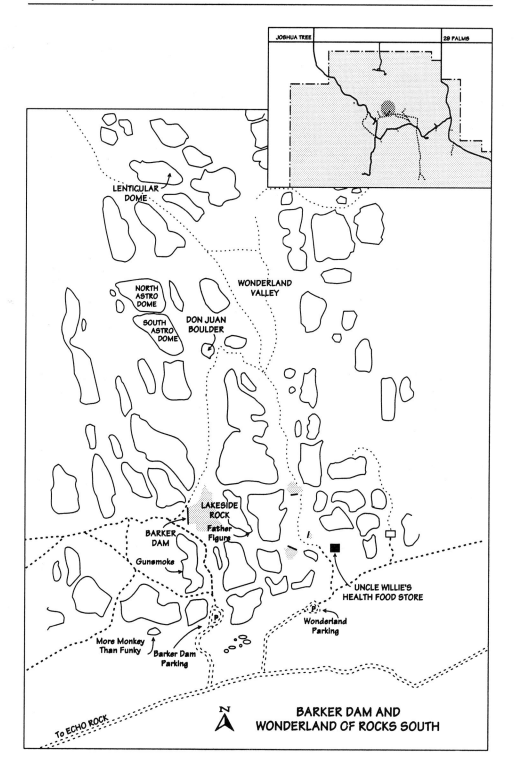

JOSHUA TREE   29 PALMS

LENTICULAR
DOME

WONDERLAND
VALLEY

NORTH
ASTRO
DOME

DON JUAN
BOULDER

SOUTH
ASTRO
DOME

LAKESIDE
ROCK

BARKER   Father
DAM   Figure

Gunsmoke

UNCLE WILLIE'S
HEALTH FOOD STORE

Wonderland
Parking

More Monkey
Than Funky   Barker Dam
               Parking

To ECHO ROCK

N

BARKER DAM AND
WONDERLAND OF ROCKS SOUTH

Barker Dam Area

To reach Barker Dam from Echo Tee, turn right and follow the Big Horn Pass Road as it heads east. After about 1 mile, turn on a side road that heads north. This road ends after about 300 yards at a large parking area. A trail (which connects with the Barker Dam Loop Trail) heads straight north to Barker Dam, about 600 yards away.

More Funky Than Monkey

This small formation lies about 200 yards west of the Barker Dam road and about 200 yards north of Big Horn Pass Road. The low formation is marked by a 20-foot roof about 30 feet off the ground. See map page 102.

131 *More Monkey than Funky* 5.11c ★★ This route can be led (using 2 ropes), but is usually top-roped. Pro: Several 1 to 3 inches.

Gunsmoke Area

To reach the Gunsmoke area from the Barker Dam parking area, head north for about 25 yards to a point where a trail heads west through some small boulders. This leads to a large, open basin extending to the west and north. The trail continues in a northwest direction and joins up with the Barker Dam Loop Trail. This excellent bouldering spot lies about 175 yards north of where the Barker Dam Loop Trail enters the open basin. Follow the trail that branches straight north from here. See map page 102.

132 *Gunsmoke* 5.11+ An excellent boulder traverse.

133 *Streetcar Named Desire* B1+ This blank stemming corner is about 25 yards south of Gunsmoke just east of the approach trail (you pass it on the way to Gunsmoke) on the northwest side of the boulder.

Barker Dam

This reservoir was constructed in the 1930s to supply much-needed water for nearby Keys Ranch. There is almost always water standing behind this concrete dam. However, drinking from or swimming in this lake is very hazardous. See map page 102.

Lakeside Rock

Just as you get to Barker Dam, a large, low-angled dome can be seen to the right (east). This is Lakeside Rock. Several 5.8 to 5.10+ face climbs are found on the steep slab facing Barker Dam. See map page 102. The following route is approached by walking right (south and then east) around the southern end of the formation.

134 *Father Figure* 5.12d ★★★ An overhanging face with 4 bolts.

Wonderland of Rocks South

The southern part of the Wonderland of Rocks lies to the north and east of Barker Dam. Although the Wonderland is one contiguous area from Willow Hole to Barker Dam, its vast size dictates that entry be made from divergent locations to provide reasonable access. Although you can also approach the southern Wonderland from Barker Dam, the most common (and easiest) way to get into this enormous area is from the Wonderland Ranch Trailhead, then up the Wonderland Valley.

Drive 200 yards on the Big Horn Pass Road past the Barker Dam turnoff; here, you'll find another turn off to the north. Follow this until it ends at a parking area. Toilets (the only ones in the area) and a trashcan are found here. Keep your impact to a minimum; use these facilities.

To reach Wonderland Valley from the parking area, head north to an old, burned-out building (Uncle Willie's Health Food Store). A wash to the left (west) of Uncle Willie's leads past a small dam to a valley that runs in a north-south direction. This is the southern end of the Wonderland Valley. See map page 102.

The Astro Domes

These two domes offer some of Joshua Tree's finest face climbing routes. The rock on the northeast faces of both the North and South Astro Domes is un-characteristically smooth. Most routes climb sharp edges or flakes on excellent rock. The Astro Domes are about 1 mile up the wash from Uncle Willie's Health Food Store. At the point where the Wonderland Valley widens, the Astro Domes will be seen about 350 yards to the northwest. A very large boulder that overhangs on all sides will be encountered on the approach, 200 yards past the point were the Wonderland Valley widens; this is the Don Juan Boulder.

South Astro Dome – Eastern Side

Descent: The easiest descent from South Astro Dome is down the northwest shoulder. This is Class 3.

135 ***Hex Marks the Poot*** (aka *Lightning Bolt Crack*) 5.7 ★★ This clean crack is located on the lower left end of the South Astro (about 80 yards left of Solid Gold.) It is easily seen on the approach (directly above Don Juan Boulder). A second pitch can be added (5.8); climb up an obvious lieback flake. Pro: To 4 inches.

136 ***My Laundry*** 5.9 ★★ Pro: Thin to 1.5 inches, 4 bolts.

137 ***Solid Gold*** 5.10a ★★★ Pro: Thin to 1.5 inches, 9 bolts.

138 ***Such a Savage*** 5.11a ★★★ Runout to the first and second bolts. Pro: 11 bolts, nuts to 1.5 inches.

South Astro Dome – Eastern Side

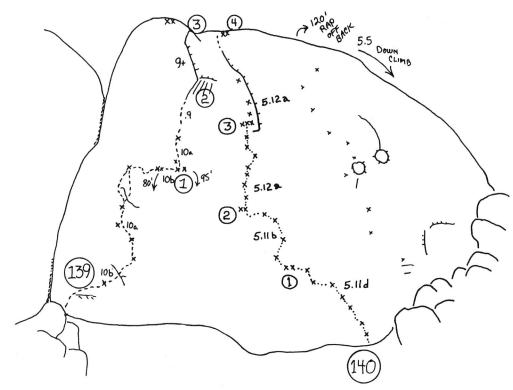

North Astro Dome – Northeast Face

Descent: The easiest descent off the North Astro Dome is down the northwest shoulder (5.4). It is possible to rappel from the belay bolts atop the routes on the west face, but two ropes are required. See map page 102.

  139 **_Figures on a Landscape_** 5.10b ★★★ Pro: 8 bolts, nuts to 3 inches.
  140 **_The Gunslinger_** 5.12a ★★★ 4 pitches. Pro: 21 bolts, nuts to 2.5 inches.

Lenticular Dome

This attractive rock lies about 450 yards north of the North Astro Dome. However, it is best approached via the main trail through the Wonderland Valley. Eventually, you must cut into a wash that heads northwest and passes directly below the southwest face of Lenticular Dome. The mottled face is characterized by a crack that ascends two-thirds up the face then stops (Mental Physics). A trail that heads north from near Don Juan Boulder leads directly into this wash and offers an alternative route.

Descent: Along the top and down and to the left, then down slabs into a gully. See map page 102.

  141 **_Dazed and Confused_** 5.9 ★★ This is the bolted face climb that starts 20 feet left of Mental Physics. 165 foot rope needed. Pro: bolts, bolt belay.
  142 **_Mental Physics_** 5.7+ ★★★ This route climbs the obvious crack in the center of the southwest face to a belay. Continue up face climbing to the top. Pro: To 3 inches, 1 bolt.

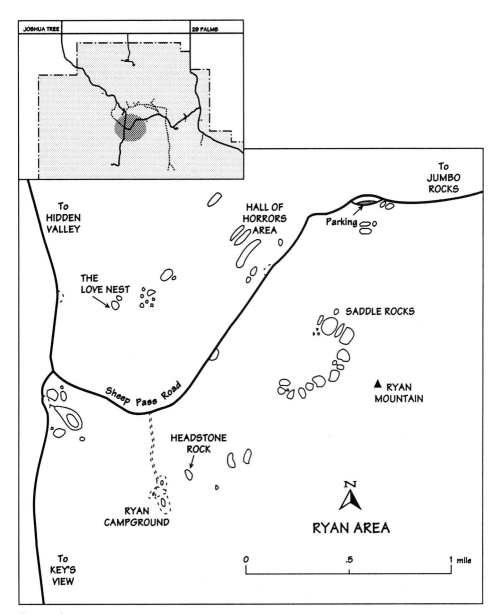

Ryan Area

The remainder of this Joshua Tree section covers crags as they are encountered along the Quail Springs Road. From Hidden Valley Campground, Quail Springs Road heads south for about 2 miles to a point where the Key's View Road branches off right. The Quail Springs Road curves east, then northeast, from here. From the point of its intersection with the Key's View Road, Quail Springs Road changes names (probably just to confuse people). For about the next 11 miles, the main road is called Sheep Pass Road.

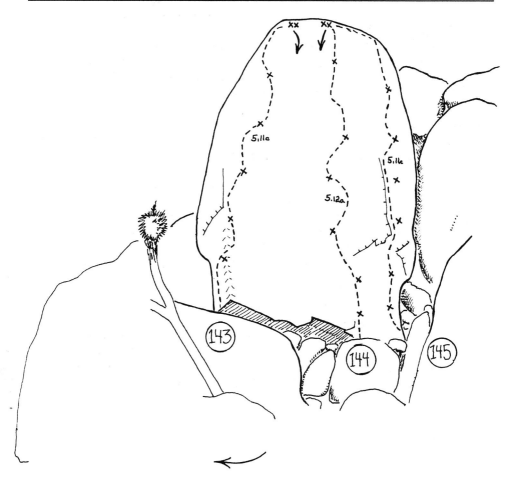

The Love Nest

This area lies about 0.3 mile east of the Quail Springs Road at a point 1.3 miles south of Hidden Valley Campground and 0.3 mile before you get to the Cap Rock/Key's View Road turnoff. This is the first set of rocks encountered as you walk east from Quail Springs Road. The three routes (Routes 173 through 175) are located on the slightly-overhanging south face of the formation. Apparently, a large number of rattlesnakes spend the winter under The Love Nest formation. Care should be taken – particularly in the spring, when the snakes emerge. Do not disturb the snakes; they soon scatter throughout the Monument when temperatures warm. See map page 107.

143 ***We Don't Need No Stinking Badges*** 5.11c ★★ Starts at the left-hand corner of the south face. Pro: 6 bolts, bolt anchors.

144 ***Boys Don't Cry*** 5.12a ★★ Climb past 6 bolts up the center of the south face. Bolt anchors.

145 ***Shakin' Like Milk*** 5.11c ★★ Start at right-hand side of face, up a small corner, then to the top. Pro: 6 bolts; shares anchor with preceding route.

Ryan Campground
Ryan Campground is located about 0.75 mile east of Cap Rock, along the Sheep Pass Loop Road. Take a dirt road about 0.25 mile south to the actual campground. A few routes are located in the campground, while the balanced pillar to the east (Headstone Rock) provides the best and most popular routes.

Headstone Rock
This pillar of rock sits on top of a jumble of rocks and boulders about 200 yards east of the campground. The first ascent of Headstone Rock was made in 1956 by Bob Boyle and Rod Smith. A rope, tossed over the summit, was climbed to reach the top. A single rope is sufficient for the rappel descent. See map page 107.

Headstone Rock – South Face
146 *SW Corner* 5.6 ★★ Start left of center of the south face, climb up and left to the arête, then to the top. Pro: 4 bolts.

147 *Cryptic* 5.8 ★★ Climb the face just left of the southeast arête past 3 bolts.

Headstone Rock – North Face
148 *The Cutting Edge* 5.13b ★ This route climbs the northeast arête of Headstone Rock. Pro: 4 bolts (some hard to clip).

149 *Headmaster* 5.12b (TR) ★★ Start in the middle of the north face; climb up and right, eventually reaching the right-hand arête below the top.

150 *Headbangers' Ball* 5.12d ★ Start just right of the northwest arête, on the west face, climb more or less straight up. Pro: 4 bolts.

Saddle Rocks

This very large slab of rock lies about 1 mile northeast of Ryan Campground, on the side of Ryan Mountain, to the east of Sheep Pass Road. A series of car pullouts on the right and left sides of Sheep Pass Road (also the parking area for the Hall of Horrors) leave about a 0.5 mile walk eastward to the rock. The Hall of Horrors is on the west side of the road. Please follow the climber trail/markers to reduce impact in this area. See map page 107.

North Face

The following routes lie on the northern and northwest part of the lower summit of Saddle Rocks. Most of these routes end at almost the same place. Descent for these routes is usually via a rappel down the northeast side of the rock (at the top of Right On).

151 *Space Mountain* 5.10b ★★ Start at a giant, left-facing open book on the northeast corner of the lower formation. This is just below the rappel route on the north end of the lower formation. Follow a traversing crack right until you can climb straight up the steep face above past bolts. Pro: Thin (for start), all bolts above (bring runners), 2-rope rappel.

152 *The Iconoclast* 5.13a ★★★ This route climbs the overhanging arête down and to the right of Space Mountain. Pro: bolts.

153 *Right On* 5.5 ★ Pro: To 3 inches.

West Face

These routes generally lie on the main/large western aspect of Saddle Rocks. These routes are all two to three pitches in length.

Descent: Several descents are possible. Many people make two double-rope rappels down Walk on The Wild Side (be careful if people are coming up that route). It is also possible to make two single-rope rappels down the southwestern part of the rock, but some downclimbing is involved. Finally, you can head down the south side of the Lower Summit (downclimb a chimney), then either downclimb slabs below or rappel.

154 *The High Cost of Living* 5.11a to 5.12a (depending on height) ★★★ Pro: Bolts, few nuts for bottom and top anchors.

155 *A Cheap Way to Die* 5.10d ★★ Pro: Bolts, few nuts for bottom.

156 *Roughriders* 5.11b ★★ Pro: 14 bolts and top anchors.

157 *Walk on the Wild Side* 5.7+ ★★★ Pro: Bolts, longer runners helpful.

Saddle Rocks
North Face and West Face

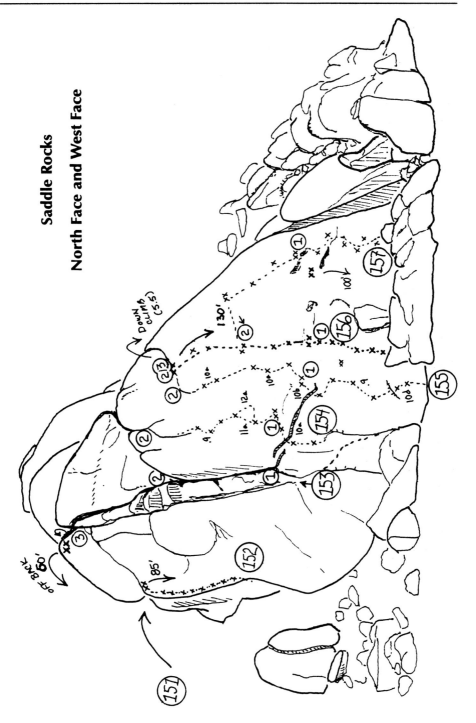

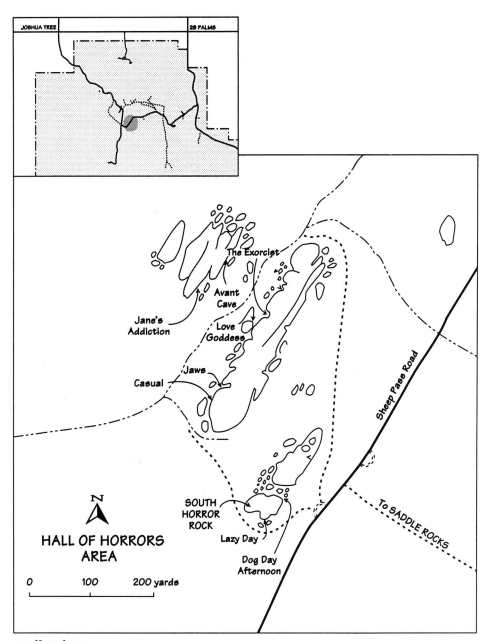

Hall Of Horrors

This fine area lies about 1 mile northeast of Ryan Campground, on west side of the Sheep Pass Road. A series of car pullouts on the right and left sides of Sheep Pass Road (also the parking area for the Saddle Rocks) will be found here. Please follow the climber trail/markers to reduce impact in this area.

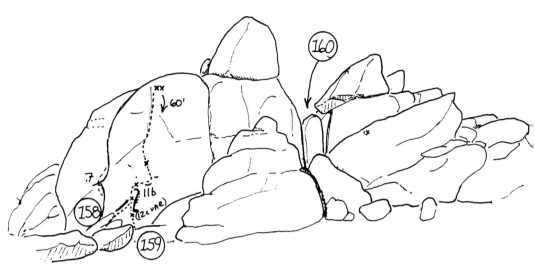

South Horror Rock

The southernmost rock, closest to the road.

  158 *Lazy Day* 5.7 ★ Pro: To 2.5 inches.
  159 *Cactus Flower* 5.11b ★★ Start on the left and traverse up and right (direct start is 5.12c). Pro: Small camming units and bolts/bolt anchor.
  160 *Dog Day Afternoon* 5.10b ★★ This route lies on the left side of the corridor, near the arête; steep face climbing. Pro: 5 bolts, medium nuts, 2-bolt anchor/rap.

Hall Of Horrors – East Wall

The main "Hall" lies west of the formation that is next to the road. Most of the established routes lie within the canyon formed by two long domes. See map page 112.

South Horror Rock
The southernmost rock, closest to the road.

158 *Lazy Day* 5.7 ★ Pro: To 2.5 inches.
159 *Cactus Flower* 5.11b ★★ Start on the left and traverse up and right (direct start is 5.12c). Pro: Small camming units and bolts/bolt anchor.
160 *Dog Day Afternoon* 5.10b ★★ This route lies on the left side of the corridor, near the arête; steep face climbing. Pro: 5 bolts, medium nuts, 2-bolt anchor/rap.

Hall Of Horrors – East Wall
The main "Hall" lies west of the formation that is next to the road. Most of the established routes lie within the canyon formed by two long domes. See map page 112.

West Face Center Routes
The next several routes are located on the center part of the west face of the east wall of the "Hall of Horrors." Several of these end on an interesting summit; the descent is somewhat tricky. The quickest (but most intimidating) way off is to walk to the left (northeast) until you must leap across a deep fissure before easier scrambling leads you to the base. More popular is a circuitous and slightly gravelly descent to the right.

161 *Nurn's Romp* 5.8 ★ Pro: To 3 inches.
162 *Exorcist* 5.10a ★★★ Somewhat of a Josh classic. Pro: Mostly thin nuts, 1 bolt; 2 to 3 inches for belay.
163 *Antichrist* 5.11a ★ The hardest move is getting off the ground; most jump for the first hold. Continue up one of the three cracks above (5.7 to 5.9). Pro: 3 bolts; 2 to 3 inches for belay.

Mayr Block Routes
The following three bolted sport routes lie on the large block 50 feet right of The Exorcist recess. Descent is via a single-rope rap off bolt anchors.

164 *Love Goddess* 5.12a ★★
165 *Moonshadow* 5.12c ★★
166 *La Cholla* 5.12d ★★

Hall Of Horrors

west face of the east wall

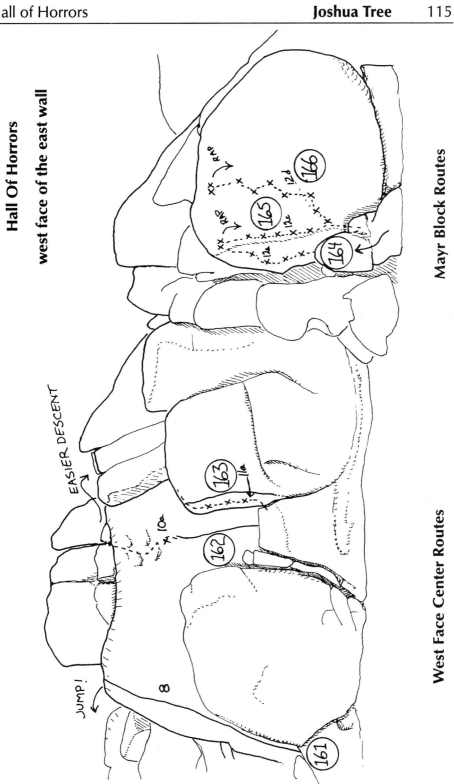

Mayr Block Routes

West Face Center Routes

West Face Right End Routes

These moderate routes lie near the extreme right-hand end of the west side of the east formation. The Right End routes all lie on a large, slabby face with a chimney near its left side. The chimney is the classic Jaws. Several routes not listed also lie on this face. See map page 112.

Descent: Downclimb boulders to the left of Buenos Aires.

167 *Buenos Aires* 5.10a A 2-bolt climb just left of the Jaws chimney. Pro: Bolts, nuts for anchor.

168 *Jaws* 5.6 R ★★ This route climbs up the chimney system on the left end of the face; above it becomes completely enclosed. Pro: To 2.5 inches.

169 *Casual* 5.9 This is the 3-bolt face climb just to the right of Jaws. Pro: Bring nuts for anchor.

170 *Doin' Life* 5.10a This is the bolted face route just right of Casual, and just left of an arching crack/flake system. Pro: Nuts for anchors.

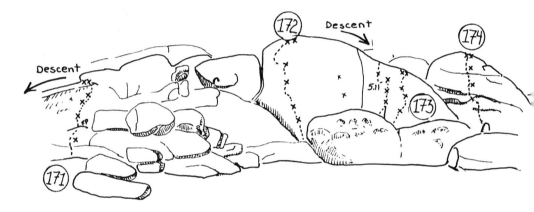

Hall of Horrors – West Wall (East Face)

A number of fine sport face routes can be found on the West Wall in the Hall of Horrors. Some need nuts for anchors. See map page 112.

171 *Jane's Addiction* 5.11b ★★★ Pro: 4 bolts, fixed pin, bolt anchor.

172 *Avant Chain* 5.12a ★ A reachy move up high may be the crux for shorter folk. Pro: 4 bolts (chain hangers), bolt anchor.

173 *Avant Cave* 5.11c ★ Pro: Small camming units, bolts, bolt anchor.

174 *Read My Flips* 5.11a Pro: Small to 2.5 inch cams, 2 bolts, 2-bolt anchor.

Geology Tour Road

A dirt road heads south from Sheep Pass Loop Road approximately 2.5 miles east of Sheep Pass Campground. This is the Geology Tour Road, so named because of the self-guided geology tour that follows this road. Several climbing areas are located both east and west of this road. The "tour" has several marked stops, numbered sequentially; these marked stops have turnouts which serve as approach parking for climbing areas. Reference to the marked stops is used to assist you in locating approach parking for specific areas. See map on facing page.

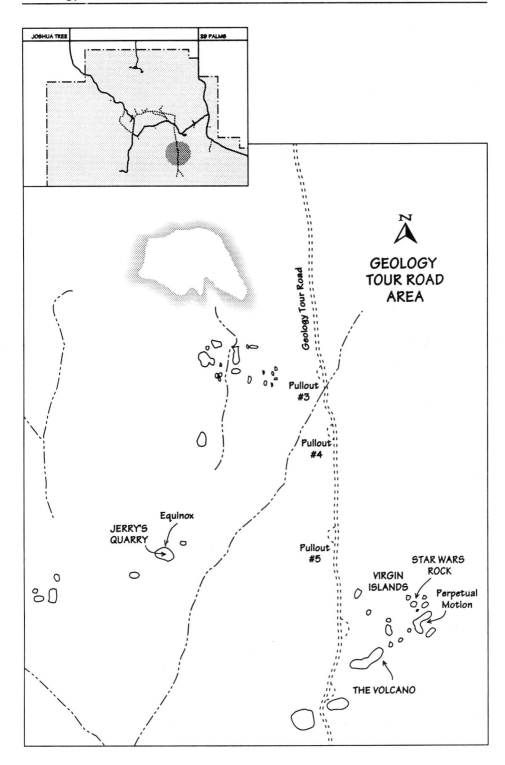

Jerry's Quarry

To approach Jerry's Quarry (a complex set of boulders and rocks on sitting high off the desert floor), park at tour marker #5 (3.7 miles south of Sheep Pass Road). Jerry's Quarry lies 0.75 mile west of the road. The northwest side of the formation has an incredible finger crack that goes up and then curves left (Equinox).

   175 *Equinox* 5.12c ★★★ Classic first- and second-knuckle finger crack. Pro: Many thin.

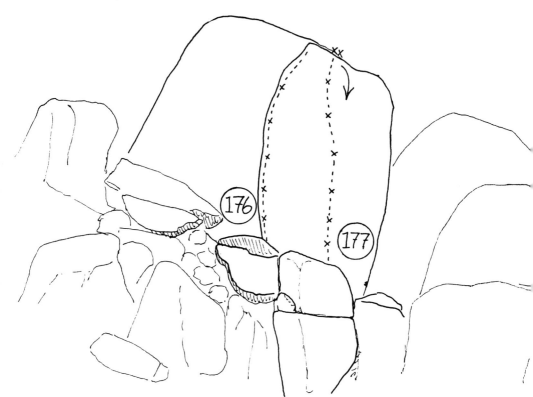

The Volcano

Several piles of rock lie to the east of the parking spot for the Lost Pencil area (about 0.75 mile south on the Geology Tour Road from Lost Pencil parking and 4.5 miles south of the Sheep Pass Loop Road). These are the Virgin Islands. The Volcano is a large rubble pile/hill east of the road. It has a number of very large boulders/rocks scattered along its slopes. The following routes lie on a large wave-shaped boulder (the Human Sacrifice Boulder) near the southeastern end of The Volcano. See map page 117.

   176 *Dictators of Anarchy* 5.12c ★★★ This route is located on the south arête of the Human Sacrifice boulder. Pro: Bolts.
   177 *New World Order* 5.13b ★★★ Just right of Dictators of Anarchy. Pro: 6 bolts; chain anchor.

Perpetual Motion Wall

A conglomeration of rubble piles lies east of The Volcano about 400 yards. This wall lies on the north side of the high, level valley (facing south) in the midst of this group. There are several approaches into this valley. See map page 117.

178 *Perpetual Motion* 5.10d ★★ Just right of the center of the Perpetual Motion Wall is this straight-in thin crack. It lies just left of two right-diagonalling chimney/off-width cracks. Pro: To 2.5 inches.

Star Wars Rock

This rock lies north of the Perpetual Motion Rubble Pile and is easily distinguished by its overhanging south face and the presence of a large split boulder to its south. See map page 117.

179 *Cedric's Deep Sea Fish Market* 5.10d ★★ This is the somewhat discontinuous thin crack to the left of and beginning below Light Sabre. Pro: Many 0.75 to 1.5 inches.

180 *Light Sabre* 5.10b ★★★ This crack route lies on the southwest face of Star Wars Rock. Start in a right-facing corner, then up thin cracks above. Pro: Several to 2 inches.

181 *Apollo* 5.12c (TR) ★★ This route lies on the overhanging south face of Star Wars Rock.

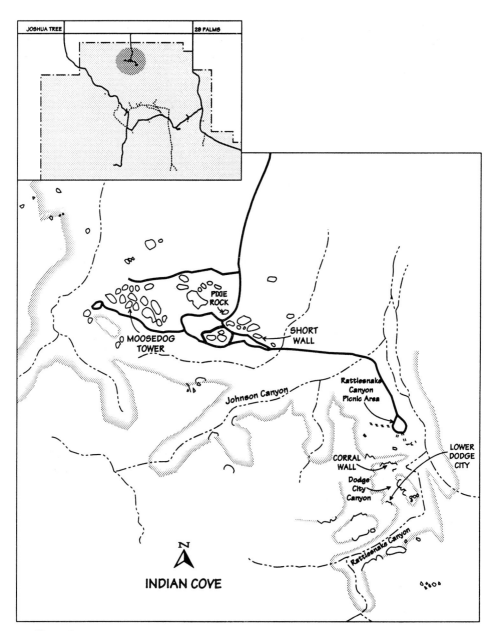

Indian Cove

This area is located along the northern edge of the monument, just south of Highway 62 (29 Palms Highway), and is effectively isolated from all other climbing areas in the monument. It is reached by driving east from the town of Joshua Tree about 9 miles. There, a small sign and some buildings point the way on the remaining three miles to Indian Cove Campground. Because of its lower altitude, Indian Cove tends to have generally warmer temperatures and is less subject to high winds.

Because so many climbs start behind campsites, the monument's "Occupied Campsite Rule" particularly applies in Indian Cove. This rule states that beginning or ending a climb in an occupied campsite is only allowed when you have the permission of the person occupying the site.

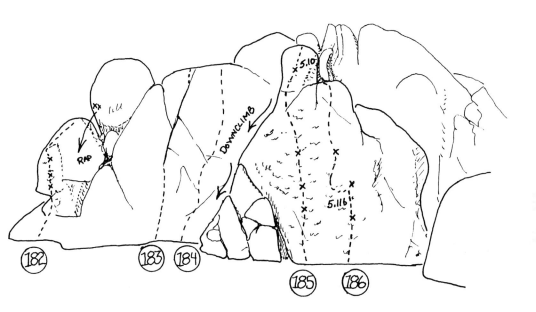

Pixie Rock

This popular rock lies just to your right (west) as you enter the campground. The right-hand edge of the south face is an extremely steep, bucketed face. To the left is a lower-angled slab.

   182 *Lascivious Conduct* 5.11c/d ★
   183 *Who's First* 5.6 R
   184 *Rhythm of the Heart* 5.8 X
   185 *Silent Scream* 5.10a ★★
   186 *Silent But Deadly* 5.11b ★

Moosedog Tower

This large, dark-colored and squarish formation lies behind campsite #91. Rappel off the north side. See map page 120.

   187 *Direct South Face* 5.9 ★★ This route climbs up a left-facing dihedral, then over a roof, on the southern (lowest) part of the rock. Three pitches up cracks and face lead to the top. Pro: Thin to 2.5 inches.
   188 *Third Time's a Charm* 5.10b ★★ Start about 60 feet uphill and left from the Direct South Face (West face); climb up easy face to a curving, shallow corner system. Follow this, pass 1 bolt, to a belay. An easy pitch leads to the top. Pro: Several thin to 2 inches.

Short Wall

This short, south-facing wall is found on the north side of the road at the east end of the campground loop. You pass it on the way to Rattlesnake Canyon. See map page 120.

Short Wall – South Face

189 *Right V Crack* 5.10a ★
190 *Linda's Face* 5.6 R
191 *Tight Shoes* 5.7 R
192 *Double Crack* 5.3 E
193 *Up To Heaven* 5.8 R/X
194 *Toe Jam Express* 5.3

195 *Steady Breeze* 5.7 X
196 *S.O.B.* 5.6
197 *Gotcha Bush* 5.4 R/X
198 *Right N Up* 5.8 X
199 *Donna T's Route* 5.5 The crack near the right end of the south face.

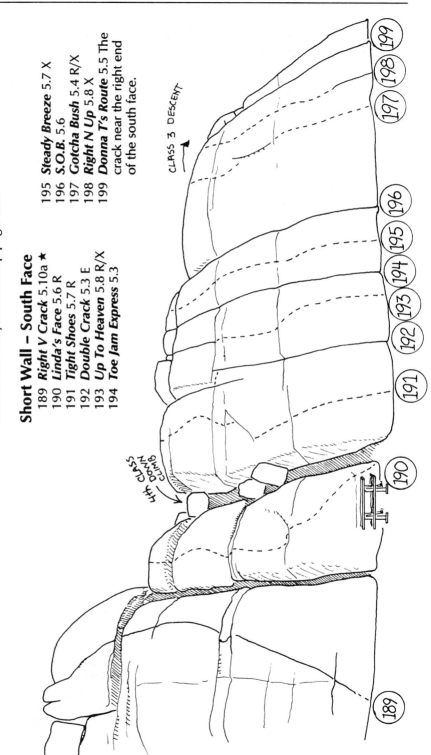

Wonderland of Rocks (Dodge City Canyon Area)

The routes and areas described are all approached from the vicinity of a picnic area about 1 mile southeast of Indian Cove Campground. Take the road heading southeast from the vicinity of The Short Wall to the picnic area, where there is parking). It is probably a good idea to examine the overview maps for this area before you start walking.

From the car, walk east to the Rattlesnake Canyon wash. Head south (up the canyon) for about 400 yards. At this point, the wash has turned to the southwest (right) and then makes an abrupt turn back east (left). The terrain becomes more jumbled past this point. When Rattlesnake Canyon turns sharply back east, head straight (southwest) up boulders through an obvious notch. Over the notch, the terrain levels, and has lots of bushes and good trails. Immediately to your right (north) is the south-facing Corral Wall. See map page 120.

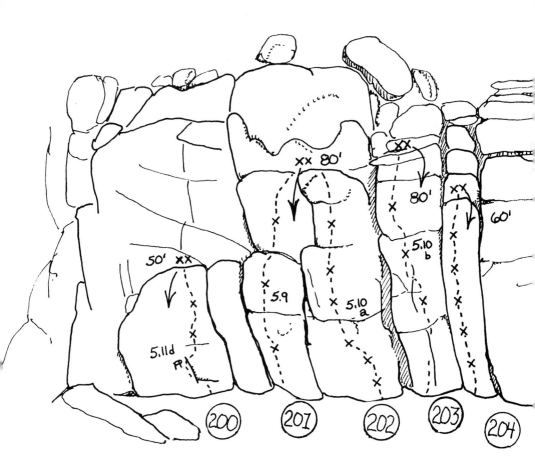

Corral Wall

This formation faces south (it is one of Josh's warmer crags), and is only about 15 minutes from the car. It is a good choice on cold or windy days. Please use consideration in leaving this and all areas in and around Rattlesnake Canyon in *better* shape than you found them. This area can get heavy use; walk on established trails. See map page 120.

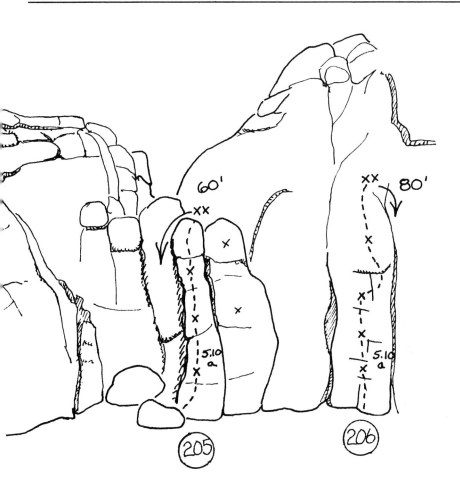

200 **Honky Justice** 5.11d ★ Pro: Thin to 1.5 inches, 2 bolts.
201 **Only Outlaws Have Guns** 5.9+ ★ Pro: 3 bolts, cams, 2-bolt anchor/rap.
202 **Six-Gun By My Side** 5.10a ★ Pro: 5 bolts, 2-bolt anchor/rap.
203 **Party In The Desert** 5.10b ★★ Pro: To 2 inches, 3 bolts, 2-bolt anchor/rap.
204 **Wild Wild West** 5.10d Stay to the left. Pro: 5 bolts.
205 **Hang 'em High** 5.10a ★ Pro: To 2 inches, 3 bolts, 2-bolt anchor/rap.
206 **Exfoliation Confrontation** 5.10a ★★ Pro: 4 bolts, 2-bolt anchor/rap.

Lower Dodge City

From the Corral Wall area, walk to near the middle of the Corral Wall, then head south up Dodge City Canyon. Stay on the left (east) side of the canyon, following a path that avoids the thick bushes. Above, boulder-hopping takes you across to the right (west) side of the canyon where this formation will be found. See map page 120.

207 ***Hangman Jury*** 5.11c ★★ This route is the lower and left-most route. 6 bolts protect face climbing past a horizontal crack. 2-bolt anchor/rap.

208 ***Frontier Justice*** 5.11b ★★★ Up and right of Hangman Jury, climb up to and then over a small roof, continue up vertical face. Pro: To 2 inches, 7 bolts, 2-bolt anchor/rap.

Bill Freeman

Rico Miledi climbing *Frontier Justice*, 5.11b

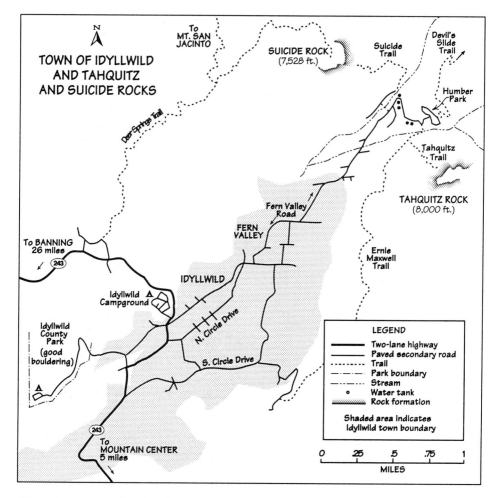

How to get to the Rocks

See the overview map of southern California on page viii which shows major road and freeway approaches to Idyllwild. From the town of Hemet, take Highway 74 for 14 miles to the junction with Highway 243 at Mountain Center. Go north 5 miles on Highway 243 to the town of Idyllwild. From the town of Banning, along US 10, take Highway 243 south for 26 miles to Idyllwild.

From the town of Idyllwild, drive up North Circle Drive (the Fern Valley road) through town to Humber Park where the road ends (see map). Humber Park is a trailhead for the San Jacinto Wilderness, and consists of a small loop road and parking area. Toilets and trash cans are the only facilities at Humber Park.

Tahquitz & Suicide

The fine granite crags of Tahquitz and Suicide Rocks are located on the high western slope of the San Jacinto mountain range in southern California, above the mountain town of Idyllwild. Climbs tend to be excellent in quality, even in the easier grades. Some loose rock can be found, but overall the climbs are superb. Tahquitz and Suicide are about an hour's drive from Joshua Tree.

Camping
Camping is not permitted at Humber Park, although climbers often bivouac in their cars anyway. There are several campgrounds within a short driving distance of Humber Park near the town of Idyllwild.

Idyllwild (County) Park is located 0.5 mile west of Idyllwild on Riverside County Playground Road, within walking distance of town. Check for amount of camping fees. Hot showers (extra) and excellent bouldering. Open year-round. Telephone (909) 659-2656.

The Idyllwild Campground is located just north of town along Highway 243 (25905 Highway 243). Summer rates are $14 per night; off-season is $12 per night. Hot showers, flush toilets, tables, etc. Reservations may be necessary in the summer. For reservations call 1-800-444-7275; the key # for the campground is 6872. Telephone for the campground is (909) 659-2607.

The Stone Creek Campground is located about 6 miles north of Idyllwild on Highway 243. Summer rates are $8 per night, winter rates $6 per night. Pit toilets, tables, fire rings, no showers.

Black Mountain Campground is located along a dirt road off Highway 243, approximately 14 miles north of Idyllwild. Excellent bouldering and a number of short sport climbs are found in the immediate area. Rates are $7 per night; no reservations taken. Open from May to October (approximately). Pit toilets, tables, fire rings, no showers.

Climbing Stores
Climbing and camping equipment can be purchased at Nomad Ventures in Idyllwild, 54415 North Circle Drive. Telephone (909) 659-4853.

Guidebooks
A comprehensive guide to Tahquitz and Suicide (*Climber's Guide to Tahquitz & Suicide*, by Randy Vogel and Bob Gaines) can be purchased at most southern California climbing stores.

Permits
Although Tahquitz and Suicide Rocks are both located in wilderness areas, currently no permit is required for climbers. Trailhead registration may be implemented in the near future.

Emergencies

In the case of a medical emergency or climbing accident, litters will be found at Lunch Rock, and at the top of the Friction Route Descent at Tahquitz, and near The Weeping Wall at Suicide Rock. Please make sure that these are returned to where they were found. For rescues, contact the Riverside Mountain Rescue Unit. They can be reached through the Riverside County Sheriff's Office by dialing 911 or 925-0456.

Equipment

Routes at both Tahquitz and Suicide can require considerable amount of traditional protection. This is particularly true for routes at Tahquitz. A good selection of nuts, from tiny brass/steel nuts to large camming devices (3 inches or more) and runners may be required. Equipment suggestions are made for many of the routes.

Descent Routes

Descents can be complicated and/or technical. The most frequently used descents are described in the text or on the topos. You may want to familiarize yourself with the descent you plan to use before starting to climb.

Tahquitz Routes (shown in photo at right)

1   *The Step* 5.9 ★
2   *Le Toit* 5.11c ★★
3   *Super Pooper* 5.10a ★★
4   *The Vampire* 5.11a ★★★
5   *The Jam Crack* 5.7 ★
6   *Dave's Deviation* 5.9 ★
7   *Piton Pooper* 5.7 ★
8   *Upper Royal's Arch* 5.7+ ★
9   *Angel's Fright* 5.5 ★
10 *Human Fright* 5.10a ★★
11 *Fred* 5.11a ★★★
12 *Blankety Blank* 5.10c ★★
13 *Fingertrip* 5.7 ★★
14 *Fingertip Traverse* 5.3 ★
15 *Jensen's Jaunt* 5.6
16 *Traitor Horn* 5.8 ★★★
17 *The Edge* 5.11a R\X ★★
17a *Turbo Flange* 5.11c R/X

FRICTION ROUTE DESCENT

THE TROUGH

LUNCH ROCK

Photo by Bob Gaines

Tahquitz Rock

Approach To Tahquitz

The normal approach to Tahquitz Rock starts on the Ernie Maxwell Trail. The trailhead is located just before the first sharp bend at Humber Park, 0.25 mile up the road from the Suicide Rock parking area. Follow the Ernie Maxwell Trail across Strawberry Creek, then proceed about 200 yards (around a bend) along this well-graded trail to a point where a very crude trail will be seen heading straight up the hillside on your left. This steep and rough trail heads about 0.4 mile up the hillside (staying right of a talus field). It eventually leads you to the base of Lunch Rock, where most climbers leave their packs, etc. Plan on 20 to 30+ minutes for the approach from the car.

Descent: The Friction Route is a class 3-4 downclimb on the southern side of Tahquitz Rock. It is the most commonly used means of descent off Tahquitz Rock. More than a few climbers have inadvertently strayed while descending, sometimes with catastrophic results. Please descend carefully, or ask other climbers familiar with the descent where it goes.

To descend via the Friction Route from the Northwest Buttress and Bulge Routes, head down and right over large boulders to where a large boulder above the South Face will be seen.

From the top of the West and South Face climbs, head up low-angle slabs (northeast) along the ridgetop of the rock. A very large boulder will be seen ahead. If you get to the larger summit blocks of Tahquitz, you have gone too far.

Shimmy down the far (northeast) side of this large boulder. Below, a series of ramps lead down and to the left of the South Face area. Lower down, head eastward (left), across slabs until the ground is reached. Hike down along the South Face. (See map, page 133.)

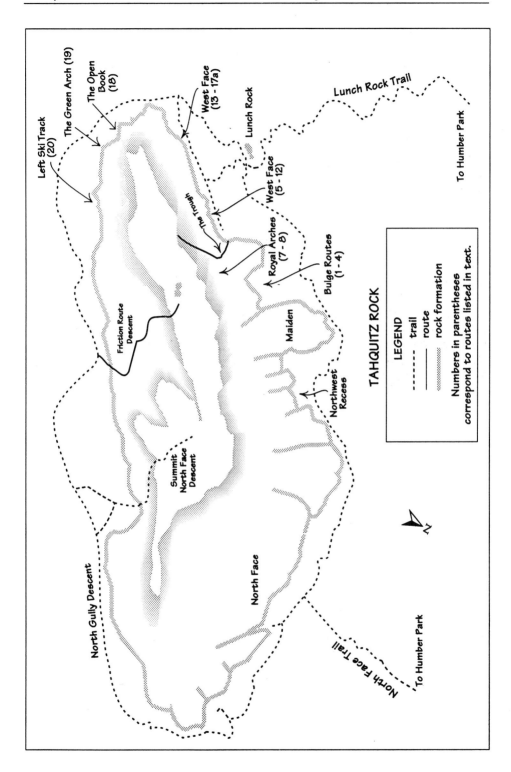

The Green Arch (19)

The Open Book (18)

West Face (13 - 17a)

Lunch Rock

Lunch Rock Trail

To Humber Park

Left Ski Track (20)

The Trough

West Face (5 - 12)

Royal Arches (7 - 8)

Bulge Routes (1 - 4)

Friction Route Descent

Maiden

Northwest Recess

LEGEND

- - - - - trail

———— route

rock formation

Numbers in parentheses correspond to routes listed in text.

TAHQUITZ ROCK

Summit North Face Descent

N

North Gully Descent

North Face

North Face Trail

To Humber Park

Bulge Routes

This section of Tahquitz Rock features the large bulging headwall on the West Face of Tahquitz Rock. This bald-looking feature hosts several excellent routes, including southern California's finest route: The Vampire 5.11a. This area includes routes on the steep rock just to the left and is bordered on the right by the large break in the rock that runs diagonally up and right (The Trough 5.0). From Lunch Rock head straight up to the base of the rock (near Angel's Fright) and traverse left along the base to The Trough gully.

The Step, Le Toit and Super Pooper start from a large ledge located above and to the left of The Trough. This ledge is best reached by climbing From Bad Traverse, a relatively easy traverse/ledge system beginning at The Trough. Easy climbing (5.0) up From Bad Traverse leads to a bushy Mountain Mahogany. A few tricky moves up and left (5.6) lead to the large ledge. To approach The Vampire, take a short crack/corner system directly above the Mountain Mahogany to a large flat ledge (5.7). Many climbers may wish a belay once the Mountain Mahogany is reached.

Descent from the top is down the Friction Route, or for very skilled climbers, down The Trough (5.0). For a description of the Friction Route Descent, see page 132.

1 *The Step* 5.9 ★ Start from the upper left side of the ledge, climbing a crack system just left of the obvious large roof of Le Toit. Pro: Small to 2.5 inches.
2 *Le Toit* 5.11c ★★ This route climbs directly over the large roof above the ledge. Start to the right, climbing up face moves past a bolt to an arch that leads to the roof. Pro: Several thin to 2.5 inches.
3 *Super Pooper* 5.10a ★★ From the ledge, climb up and right up easy ledges to establish a belay. A long crux pitch leads to a good ledge. Pro: Thin to 3 inches.
4 *The Vampire* 5.11a ★★★ Climb a short pitch directly up from the Mountain Mahogany on From Bad Traverse (5.7) to a ledge. From the right side of the ledge, climb down slightly to reach a hand crack. Belay either at a small ledge or at double bolts that protect the crux of the second pitch. Pro: Small wires, many cams to 3 inches.

7 and 8 – see pages 136 and 137

West Face Area

This section of rock is bordered on the left side by the large break in the rock that runs diagonally up and right (The Trough, 5.0) and on the left by The Edge. The Edge is the left side of the huge dihedral of The Open Book. This section of rock lies directly above the vicinity of Lunch Rock. The routes on this section of rock seem to share (converge upon) several final pitches of rock leading to the top. Routes tend to end on The Trough or Lunch Ledge (a ledge with a solitary pine directly above Lunch Rock).

Descent: Usually via the Friction Route (see page 132), although very skilled climbers will downclimb The Trough (5.0). It is also possible to rappel from Lunch Ledge via several small trees (a single rope will suffice, but two ropes recommended). Finally, a double-rope rappel is possible from the first pitch of Fred, and two single-rope rappels are possible from the second pitch of Blankety Blank.

Bulge Routes

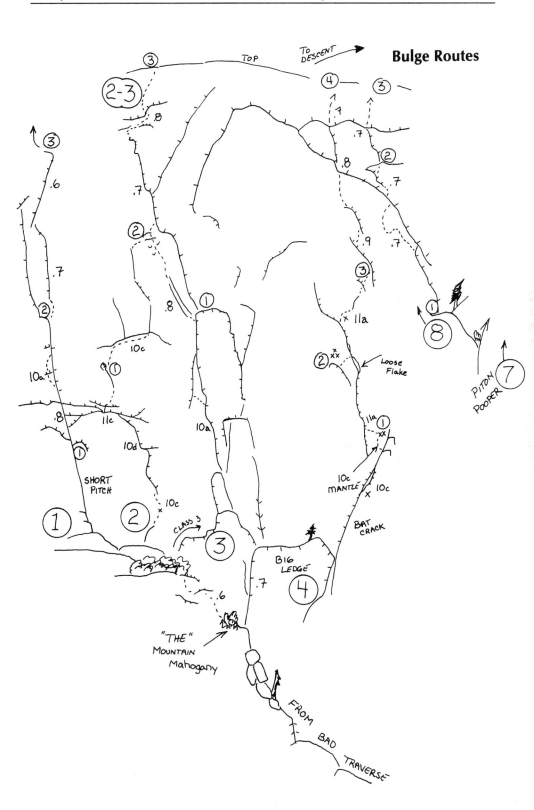

West Face

To approach Jam Crack through Blankety Blank: from Lunch Rock, head straight up to the base of the rock (near Angel's Fright/Human Fright); traverse right or left along the base. To approach Fingertrip through The Edge, head right from Lunch Rock to where the base of the rock comes down to meet the trail.

5   ***The Jam Crack*** 5.7 ★ This route starts just to the right of the start of The Trough in a small corner/crack system. This route ends on a large ledge on The Trough, below the Summit. Climb Piton Pooper or continue up The Trough to the top. Pro: Thin to 2.5 inches.

6   ***Dave's Deviation*** 5.9 ★ Start as per The Jam Crack, but head up and right on flakes to a mountain mahogany growing out of a thin hand crack. After the first pitch it is best to continue up The Jam Crack. Pro: Thin to 2 inches.

7   ***Piton Pooper*** 5.7 ★ This climb starts above the ledge where The Jam Crack and Dave's Deviation end. It starts at the extreme left end of this ledge in a small left-facing corner. Pro: Thin to 2 inches. (Also see topo page 135.)

8   ***Upper Royal's Arch*** 5.7+ ★ This route provides a more interesting finish to Piton Pooper. After the first pitch of Piton Pooper, you may want to move the belay up and left. Lots of exposure! Pro: Thin to 2 inches. (Also see topo page 135.)

9   ***Angel's Fright*** 5.5 ★ Start almost directly above Lunch Rock; the first pitch climbs a short chimney to a bushy ledge. Above, head up and right to reach the left-tending crack/corner system which marks this route. Pro: 0.5 to 2.5 inches.

10   ***Human Fright*** 5.10a ★★ Start almost directly above Lunch Rock; the first pitch climbs a clean crack up to right-facing, huge flakes/cracks. Pro: Thin, several 1 to 2 inches.

11   ***Fred*** 5.11a ★★★ Start just right of a large pine growing at the base, almost directly above Lunch Rock, climbing up moderate face to a large jammed flake. Many climbers rap off after the first pitch (100 feet). The second pitch eases after the third bolt and joins Fingertrip. Pro: Thin to 1 inch; 6 bolts.

12   ***Blankety Blank*** 5.10c ★★ Head up from Lunch Rock to the base, head right and then follow the base down slightly for about 40 feet. A small arch above a smooth face marks the start. Two single or one double-rope rappel is possible from top of second pitch. Third pitch leads to Lunch Ledge. Pro: Several thin to 1 inch.

13   ***Fingertrip*** 5.7 ★★ From Lunch Rock, head right along a trail of sorts to where the base of the rock comes down to meet the trail. The first pitch starts in a shallow red-stained corner, up and left of where the trail meets the rock. A large fir is located atop the long first pitch. A traverse left on the second pitch gives access to an arch system above the slab of Blankety Blank. Pro: Thin to 2 inches.

14   ***Fingertip Traverse*** 5.3 ★ From Lunch Rock follow the trail to the right, past the point where the rock meets the trail. Four trees stand close together ahead. Above and to the left, Class 3 climbing heads up a gully with mountain mahogany to a large pine tree near the top; the route starts here. Climb the pine until you can head left into a crack above an overhang. Pro: To 2 inches.

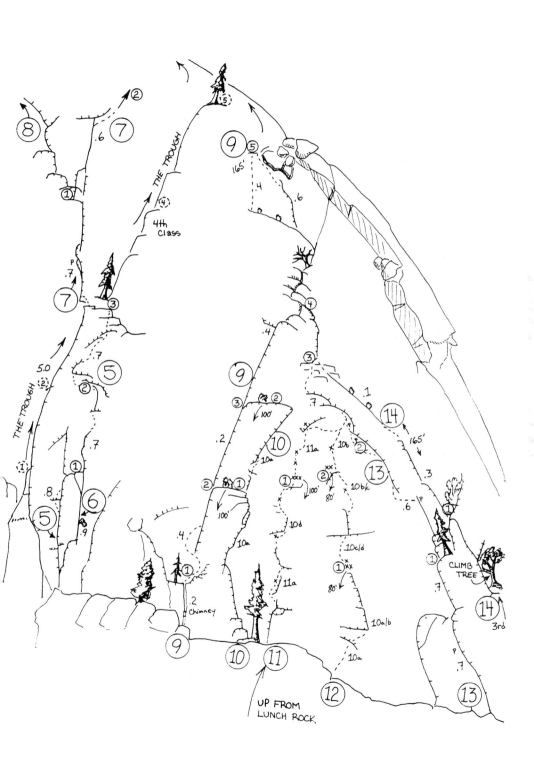

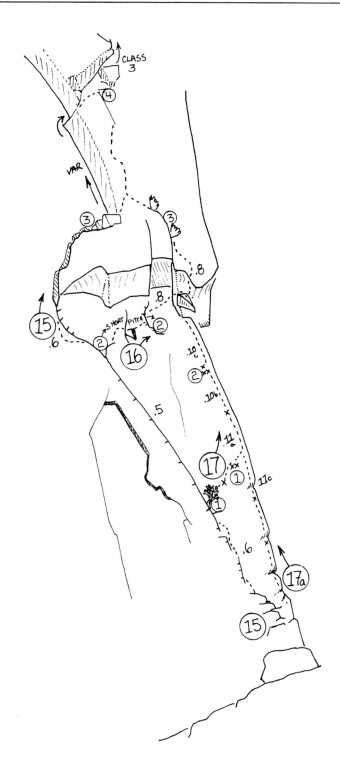

15   *Jensen's Jaunt* 5.6 This route starts at the southwest "toe" of the rock, just
      left of the sharp edge of the West Face. Head up easy blocky rock until a
      prominent crack can be reached. Pro: To 3 inches.
16   *Traitor Horn* 5.8 ★★★ Start as per Jensen's Jaunt, climbing that route for 2
      pitches until you can head right below the headwall to the "horn." Pro: Thin
      to 2.5 inches.
17   *The Edge* 5.11a R/X ★★ Start as per Jensen's Jaunt. After the first pitch head
      out right to the "edge." Finish on Traitor Horn. Pro: Very little, thin to 2
      inches, bolts.
17a   *Turbo Flange* 5.11c R/X Direct start to The Edge.

South Face Area

This section covers all the routes to the right of and including The Open Book. The
Open Book is the huge dihedral forming the southwest corner of Tahquitz. It is the
single most prominent feature on the rock. To approach the South Face area, walk
south from Lunch Rock on the rough trail that runs along the base of the rock.
Approach for routes on the south side of the Summit Block requires one to walk
past the Friction Route Descent Area then scramble up slabs (Class 3-4) to the base.
(See Overview Map, page 133.)

Descent: For South Face routes, descent is usually via the Friction Route (detailed
on page 132). For routes lying on the south face of the Summit Blocks, an easy
scramble down to the notch between Tahquitz and the mountainside above will
give access to a trail running down the south side of the rock.

18   *Open Book* 5.9 ★★★ This route follows the huge right-facing dihedral just
      around the corner from the West Face. The Edge climbs the left-hand arête
      formed by the Open Book dihedral. One of the best and most obvious routes
      on the rock. The first pitch face climbs up a slight overhang to the right of the
      crack. Pro: Thin and several up to 3 to 4 inches.
19   *Green Arch* 5.11b/c ★★ This route starts about 30 feet right of The Open
      Book. Look for the obvious right-facing and right-arching corner system which
      starts about 70 feet off the ground. 1. There are 2 variations (both 5.10) to
      gain the ledge at the base of the arch: one starts 25 feet right of Open Book
      at a large horn and the other starts about 15 feet further right. 2. Where the
      arch curves right, step right and climb up to a bolt belay. 3. Climbs the less
      steep face past 3 bolts to a 2-bolt belay ledge. 4. A 5.5 pitch leads to the top.
      (Variation, Pitch 2: from a point below where the arch curves right, it is
      possible to climb out left (5.7).) Pro: Many thin to 1.5 inches.
20   *Left Ski Track* 5.6 ★★ This route is located about 100 feet right and around
      the corner from The Open Book. Two parallel cracks in the middle of the
      South Face will be seen. 1. Start beneath the right-hand crack, climb up onto a
      sloping platform, then climb left onto the face between the cracks on
      unbelievably good jugs to a belay on a small ledge about 100 feet up. 2.
      Climb the left crack to its end at a small ledge with a fixed pin; the classic
      "step-around" move takes you around the corner to the right to a series of
      ledges; belay on the third ledge. 3. An awkward crack leads up to a fourth
      ledge; move left up an 8-foot vertical wall with double cracks to a class 4
      ledge that leads left to the top. Several variations exist from the second pitch.
      Pro: To 2.5 inches.

Approach to Suicide

The trail up to Suicide begins almost directly across Fern Valley Road from the first large water tanks encountered on the way to Humber Park (a small building is located in front). This is about 0.25 mile before you get to Humber Park. Park along Fern Valley Road (avoid "No Parking" areas) or along a side road (running south) just below the water tanks. Walk down the hillside along the trail, cross the creek, then head up to a paved road (Forest Haven Drive). Follow Forest Haven Drive all the way to its end (dirt). At this point a climbers' trail heads off right (northwest) which eventually leads to the base of Suicide Rock near The Buttress of Cracks and The Weeping Wall. Plan on 15 to 25+ minutes for the approach.

Kevin Powell

Mike Waugh on *Insomnia*.

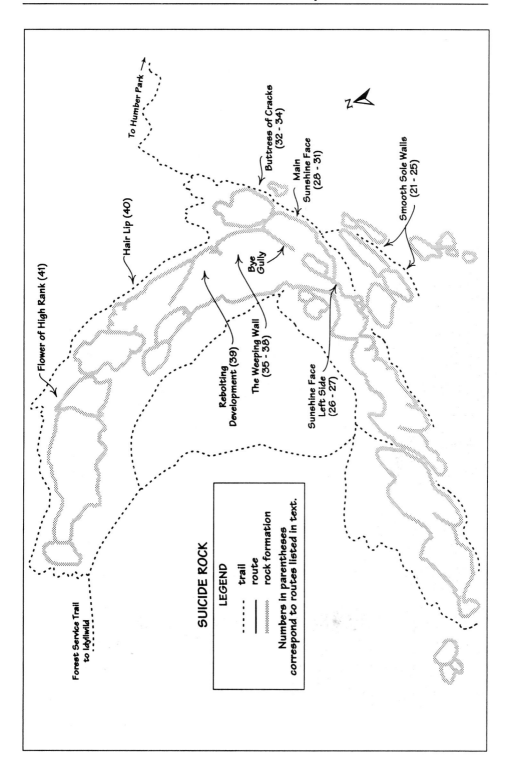

Suicide Routes (on photo page 143)

21   *Blown Out* 5.10d .
22   *Down and Out* 5.10c ★★
23   *Drowned Out* 5.10a
24   *The Fiend* 5.9 R ★
25   *Mickey Mantle* 5.8 R ★★
26   *The Man Who Fell to Earth* 5.11a ★★
27   *Caliente* 5.12c ★★
28   *Iron Cross* 5.11a ★★★
29   *Sundance* 5.10b ★★★
30   *Valhalla* 5.11a ★★★
31   *Hesitation* 5.10a ★
33   *Double Exposure* 5.10b, A1 or 5.12a ★★
35   *Surprise* 5.8 R
36   *Revelation* 5.10a ★
37   *Serpentine* 5.9 ★★
38   *Ten Karat Gold* 5.10a R ★★
39   *Rebolting Development* 5.11a R? ★
40   *Hair Lip* 5.10a ★★
41   *Flower of High Rank* 5.9 ★★

Photo by Bob Gaines

Smooth Sole Walls

The Smooth Sole Walls are located to the left and below the large Sunshine Face of Suicide and face southeast. They are comprised of two slabs split by a chimney system (Chatsworth Chimney); a large block/pillar sits atop the Smooth Sole Walls (Limp Dick). From the point where the trail up to Suicide meets the base of the rock (at the right side of The Buttress of Cracks), head left along the base of both the Buttress of Cracks and the large Sunshine Face. Where the trial steepens and begins to head up a gully, traverse left along a ledge, then under a wedged boulder to reach the base of the Smooth Sole Walls.

Left Side

Descent: Walk/downclimb to the left.

21 *Blown Out* 5.10d From the ground, climb straight up. Pro: 4 bolts; bring slings and nuts for anchors.
22 *Down and Out* 5.10c ★★ Near the right side of the left face, climb up a crack to a ledge, then up and left past a bolt. Pro: 6 bolts; slings and nuts for anchors.
23 *Drowned Out* 5.10a Near the right side of the left face, climb up a crack to a ledge, then go right up the ledge until a move up into a pocket leads to a bolt. Somewhat runout. Pro: 3 bolts; slings and nuts.

Right Side

Descent: Rap off bolt/chain anchor above at the belay ledge (80+ feet).

24 *The Fiend* 5.9 R ★ Start near the extreme left part of the right face, in a small hole, behind a boulder. Pro: 4 bolts.
25 *Mickey Mantle* 5.8 R ★★ Start left of the middle of the face (20 feet left of The Fiend). Easy mantles lead up to first bolt. Pro: 3 bolts.

Smooth Sole Walls

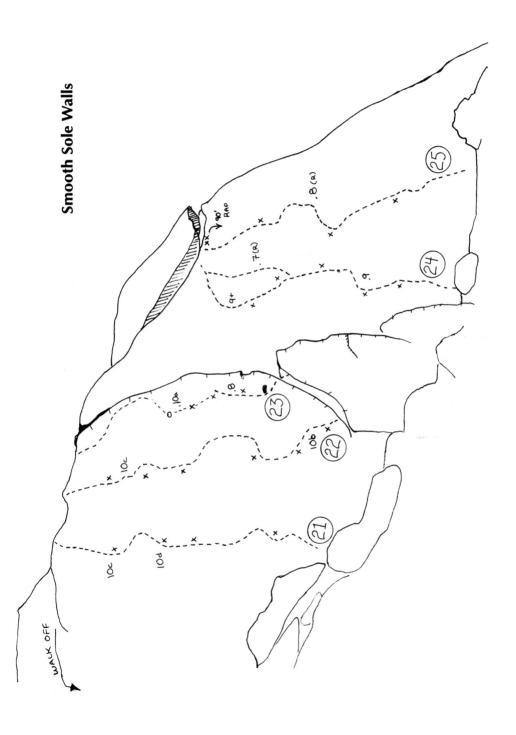

The Sunshine Face

This is the largest face at Suicide; it faces southeast. In the summer, it will be in the shade in the late afternoon. The Sunshine Face has a large block sitting at its top (Paisano Pinnacle), and a large chimney system near its left side (Paisano Chimney). From the point where the trail up to Suicide meets the base of the rock (at the right side of The Buttress of Cracks), head left along the base of the Buttress of Cracks; a short uphill scramble will lead to the Sunshine Face.

The Sunshine Face: Left Side

Walk along the base of the main Sunshine Face, then up the rock-filled gully. Go past the point where a deep chimney (Paisano Chimney) makes an obvious break in the Sunshine Face. The Left Side of the Sunshine Face lies below and left of Paisano Pinnacle.

Descent: Walk down and right to rappel anchors on a slab across from the top of Paisano Pinnacle. A single rope gives access to a large ledge (the top of the main Sunshine Face); below, downclimb a gully/chimney (Bye Gully; easy fifth-class) to the base.

26 ***The Man Who Fell to Earth*** 5.11a ★★ Class 3 climbing leads up a series of ledges to the start of the route, a shallow discontinuous thin crack. Pro: 4 bolts, thin to 1.5-inch cams.

27 ***Caliente*** 5.12c ★★ About 40 feet left of Paisano Chimney, Class 3 climbing leads up and right to a ledge/ramp. Set up the belay here. Pro: 7 bolts, thin to 2 inches.

Main Sunshine Face

All the following routes lie on the main section of the Sunshine Face, to the right of Paisano Chimney.

Descent: Downclimb the gully/chimney behind you and to the right (Bye Gully); it leads down to the base of the Weeping Wall.

28 ***Iron Cross*** 5.11a ★★★ There are two possible starts to this route. The first involves heading up the gully to the left a short distance to reach a broad ledge which can be traversed back right to the base of a large block. An alternative (which may involve more rope drag), starts as per Sundance, but heads up and slightly left to the right side of the block. Pro is a little tricky on the first pitch. Pro: 7 bolts, many thin, up to 1.5 inch.

29 ***Sundance*** 5.10b ★★★ Near the left side of the main face, below the rock filled gully, scramble up to a broad ledge. Sundance starts in a small corner system directly above. A traverse right leads to a wide crack/flake. Pro: 11 bolts, nuts to 3.5 inches.

30 ***Valhalla*** 5.11a ★★★ This route starts on a broad ledge 30 feet above the ground near the center of the Sunshine Face. The route starts a short distance right of a small pine tree on the ledge. Pro: 13 bolts, some small to medium nuts.

31 ***Hesitation*** 5.10a ★ This route starts out of a deep chimney formed by the juncture of the Sunshine Face on the left and the Buttress of Cracks on the right. Work your way up the chimney (hard at the bottom) for about 60 feet. A ramp heads up and left out of the chimney at this point. Pro: 4 bolts, small to 2 inches.

The Buttress of Cracks

The Buttress of Cracks is the lowest point of Suicide Rock, and the approach trail ends near its right side. From the point where the trail up to Suicide meets the base of the rock, head left along the base of the Buttress of Cracks; a short uphill scramble will lead to a small flat spot near the left end of the Buttress (The Pirate, a very thin straight crack, starts here). The Sunshine Face lies just around the corner to the left.

Descent: Climb up, then right along the summit, then down a notch toward the base of the Weeping Wall.

32 **Insomnia** 5.11b/c ★★★ This route lies around the corner from the small flat spot (The Pirate). Climb up the deep chimney formed by the juncture of the Buttress of Cracks and the Sunshine Face for about 25 feet. Insomnia is the nice crack on the left wall directly above. Pro: Many 1 to 2 inches.

33 **Double Exposure** 5.10b, A1 or 5.12a ★★ This route ascends the sharp arête formed by the left edge of the Buttress of Cracks and has two distinct starts. The original starts around the corner from the Pirate, using a shoulder stand and aid from 2 bolts to reach the arête. The other climbs the arête directly past bolts. Pro: Bolts, some medium nuts.

34 **The Pirate** 5.12c ★ This is the very obvious very thin crack that starts off the flat spot near the left end of the Buttress of Cracks. Pro: Many thin nuts and cams.

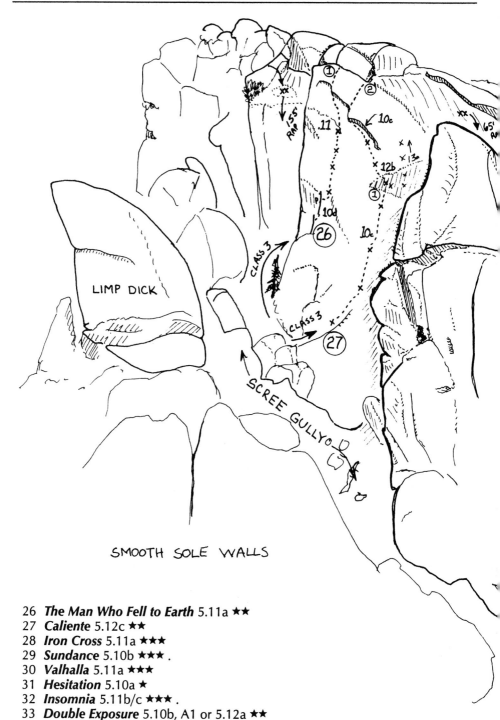

26 *The Man Who Fell to Earth* 5.11a ★★
27 *Caliente* 5.12c ★★
28 *Iron Cross* 5.11a ★★★
29 *Sundance* 5.10b ★★★ .
30 *Valhalla* 5.11a ★★★
31 *Hesitation* 5.10a ★
32 *Insomnia* 5.11b/c ★★★ .
33 *Double Exposure* 5.10b, A1 or 5.12a ★★
34 *The Pirate* 5.12c ★

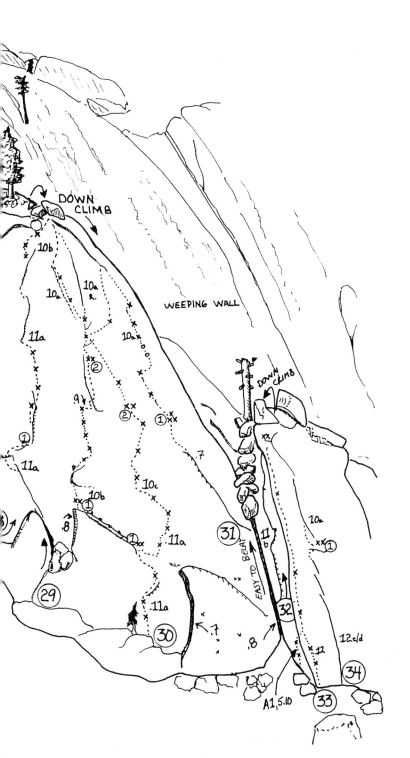

The Weeping Wall

The 300-foot Weeping Wall faces east and receives morning sun and afternoon shade. From the point where the trail up to Suicide meets the base of the rock (at the right side of The Buttress of Cracks), head up and right about 50 yards to reach the base of the Weeping Wall. The deep break/chimney on the left side of the face (Bye Gully) is the lower part of the standard descent route.

Descent: Head left along the top of the wall then up and across slabs. Downclimb to rap anchors on the slabs across from the top of Paisano Pinnacle. A single rope (65-foot rappel) gives access to a large ledge (the top of the Sunshine Face); below, downclimb Bye Gully (easy fifth-class) to the base. Alternatively, you can walk up and right along the summit of the rock until you reach a trail. Near the north end of the rock, cut down off the main rail to the base of the North Face.

35 *Surprise* 5.8 R Start at a very small crack/corner left of the center of the base, then head up and left. Pro: Bolts, small to 2 inches.

35a *Surprise Direct* 5.9 (Var. to last pitch)

35b *Duck Soup* 5.10c (see topo)

36 *Revelation* 5.10a ★ Start as per Surprise, but head up and right, using the third bolt of Serpentine, then going straight up. Pro: 12 bolts, thin to 2 inches.

37 *Serpentine* 5.9 ★★ Start next to the large oak tree near the right side of the base. A short crack leads to face climbing up and left. At the third bolt go right. Pro: 11 bolts, thin to 2 inches.

38 *Ten Karat Gold* 5.10a R ★★ From the large oak near the right side of the face, Class 3 climbing up a groove leads to a ledge; start off the left edge of this ledge. Pro: 6 bolts, medium nuts.

38a *Direct Finish* 5.10a (See topo)

39 *Rebolting Development* 5.11a R? ★ This route lies on the narrow face just right of the Weeping Wall. Start near the right side of the face. A bit runout on first pitch past second bolt. Pro: 9 bolts, nuts for anchor.

Northeast and North Face Routes

The following two routes lie some distance to the right of the Weeping Wall. Hike up to the base of the Weeping Wall, then head right along the base of the crag. (See map page 141.)

40 *Hair Lip* 5.10a ★★ This route is located approximately 60 yards right of the Weeping Wall. Look for a right-arching, very flared chimney located on the left margin of a 100-foot slab. This route starts 15 feet left of this chimney. (See map page 141.) Climb up a thin flake, then traverse left to and then up the very exposed edge. Pro: 3 bolts, thin to medium nuts.

41 *Flower of High Rank* 5.9 ★★ This route lies about 100 yards to the right of Hair Lip (160 yards right of the Weeping Wall), near the northern end of Suicide Rock. A giant right-facing dihedral containing a chimney (Cat's Cave Inn) separates the main north face from a buttress to the left. This route lies just left of Cat's Cave Inn, on the buttress, following a thin crack straight up to a large pine tree growing out of the crack some 75 feet off the ground. (See map page 141.) Pro: Many 1 to 2.5 inches.

The Weeping Wall

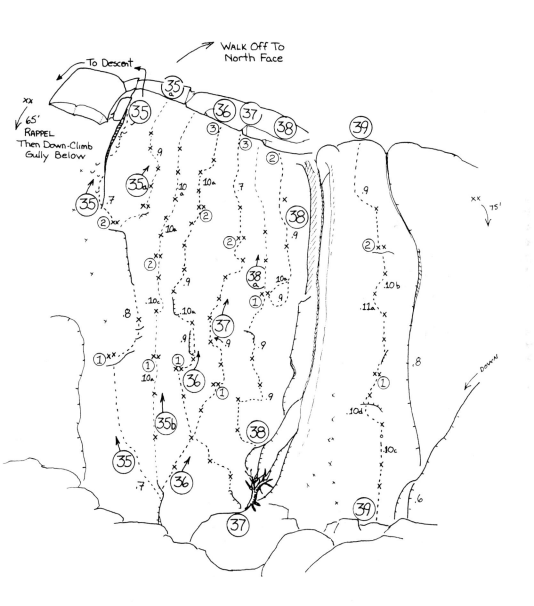

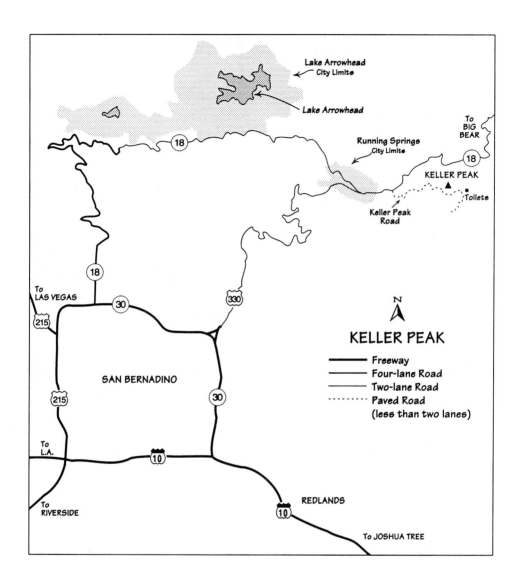

Keller Peak

Although Keller Peak has only 20 or so climbs, it is worthy of a day visit for the fun, short sport routes on the rough, overhanging granite. During the summer, it is not uncommon to find climbers on nearly every climb. Before Williamson Rock was developed, Keller Peak was the only summer sport climbing in southern California. Climbs range from 5.8 to 5.12d, with most routes in the 5.10c to 5.12a category. Several other crags have been developed in this area, but they do not offer the same concentration of good routes.

How to get to Keller Peak
Keller Peak is located mere steps from the road at an elevation of 7,500 feet. From to 10 or 215 Freeways, take Highway 30 to the Highway 330 exit. Follow Highway 330 into the mountains to the town of Running Springs (Highway 18 intersects here). Continue past Running Springs (now on Highway 18) for about 1 mile to Keller Peak Road (on your right). Follow the narrow and winding Keller Peak Road for 3.5 miles; the crag is on your left.

Season
Keller Peak is a warm-weather climbing area (April to October). During the hot summer, the crag is in the shade in the afternoon. Keller Peak Road is closed during the winter.

Equipment
Quickdraws, a few long runners and a lead rope. All the routes can be top-roped if desired.

Guidebooks
Guide to Sport Crags in Southern California by Troy Mayr covers Keller Peak and several other areas (Williamson, Devil's Punchbowl, etc.) in great detail and is recommended.

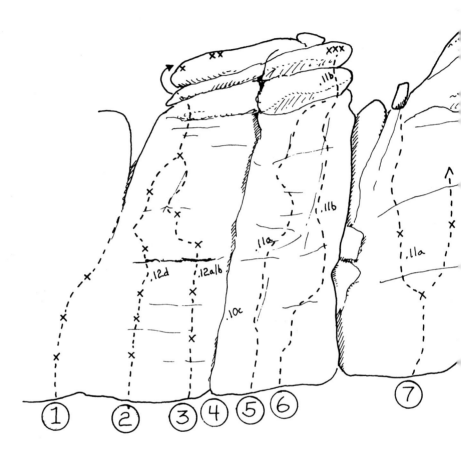

1 *Three Stooges* 5.11d
2 *Eve of the Ring* 5.12d ★★
3 *Orange Tapestry* 5.12a/b ★★★
4 *More Punk than Funk* 5.10b/c
5 *Joe's Problem* 5.11a (TR) ★
6 *Buckets To Somewhere* 5.11b (TR) ★
7 *High Spark of Low Heeled Boys* 5.11a
8 *Gravitational Humiliation* 5.11c ★★

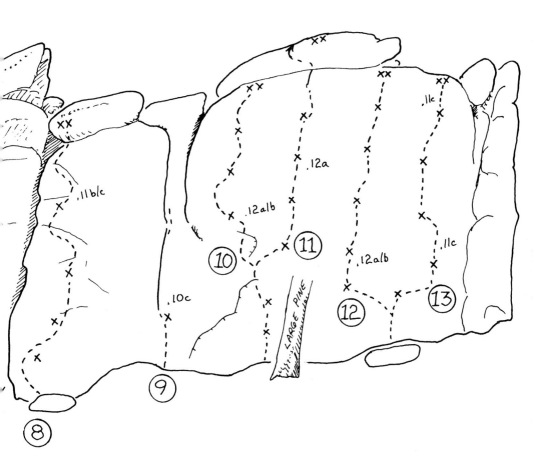

9 *Boilermaker* 5.10c
10 *Particle Accelerator* 5.12a/b ★★★
11 *Suspended Animation* 5.12a ★★
12 *Conscious Projection* 5.12a/b
13 *Segments of Space* 5.11c ★★

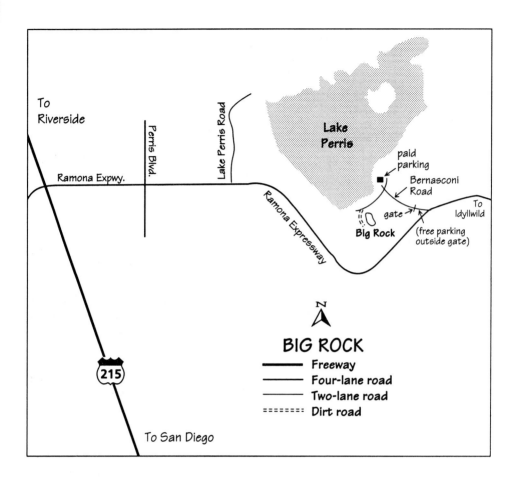

To
Riverside

Perris Blvd.

Lake Perris Road

Lake
Perris

Ramona Expwy.

Ramona Expressway

paid
parking

Bernasconi
Road

To
Idyllwild

gate

Big Rock

(free parking
outside gate)

215

To San Diego

N

BIG ROCK

━━━━━ Freeway
───── Four-lane road
───── Two-lane road
═════ Dirt road

Big Rock

Big Rock is a large granite slab (some 170 feet high) located next to a large reservoir (Lake Perris) south of the city of Riverside. The climbing is almost entirely low-angle face climbing with bolt protection. Most routes lie in the 5.4 to 5.10 category, with a few 5.11s. It is popular with beginning and intermediate climbers; its picnic tables and easy approach prove attractive for family and school outings.

How to get to Big Rock

From US 215 take the Ramona Expressway east for about 6.5 miles (past the entrance to the Lake Perris Recreation Area) to Bernasconi Road. Turn left here. You can either park for free a short distance up the road, outside the gate (warning: car break-ins are common here), or another 0.25 mile further down the road at a parking lot (entrance fee required).

From the vicinity of the parking lot mentioned above, follow a paved road west (to the left) for about 0.5 mile to a picnic area at the base of the Rock. A toilet and some climber information is also available. Camping (fee required) is also available.

Season

Best temperatures are found from October to June. It can be quite warm in the summer, but climbing is possible year-round. The crag faces to the west; it is in the shade in the morning and gets sun all afternoon.

Equipment

Quickdraws (most routes are bolted), runners, 165-foot rope. However, some climbs do require nuts for protection and/or anchors, so a selection is advisable.

Guidebooks

Other routes and bouldering can be found in this area as well. For more information consult: *Sport Crags in Southern California* by Troy Mayr and *Southern California Bouldering Guide* by Craig Fry.

Routes

Several other routes are to be found to the right of Puppy Dog (Route 20) as well as on a short, steep headwall above and left of the top of the Rock.

Descent: An easy (Class 2/3) walk-off to the left is possible from the top of the slab.

  1 *Top-rope Problem* 5.10d Pro: 2 bolts.
  2 *Edger Sanction* 5.10a/b ★ Pro: 3 bolts.
  3 *Rat Crack* 5.9
  4 *Unknown* 5.10b Pro: 3 bolts.
  5 *English Hanging Gardens* 5.11d Stick clip first bolt. Pro: 4 bolts.
  6 *Raw Deal* 5.11b ★ Start as per Jolly Green Giant, but go left at first bolt. Pro: 6 bolts.
  7 *Jolly Green Giant* 5.10c ★ Pro: 3 bolts.
  8 *Giant Step* 5.10b/c ★ Best to go right from first bolt of Jolly Green Giant; or go directly up (a little runout). Pro: 3 or 4 bolts.
  9 *Northwest Passage* 5.9+ ★★ Pro: 3 bolts (optional pro can be placed under the roof).
10 *The Roof* 5.9 ★ Pro: 4 bolts.
11 *Boogaloo* 5.9 Pro: 4 bolts.
12 *Underdog* (aka *Boogaloo Direct*) 5.9 Pro: 3 bolts.
13 *Wedunett* 5.6 Pro: 3 bolts.
14 *Crater Maker* 5.7 Pro: 2 bolts.
15 *The Trough* 5.5 ★ Pro: 9 bolts. (Can be done in one 165-foot pitch)
16 *Africa Flake* 5.6 ★ Pro: 6 bolts. (1 or 2 pitches)
17 *Super Star* (aka *Frontal Lobotomy/Long John Silver*) 5.10a Pro: 2 bolts.
18 *Mind Bender* 5.9 ★ Pro: 3 bolts.
19 *Tombstone* (aka *Pudnurtle*) 5.8 Pro: 2 bolts.
20 *Puppy Dog* 5.6 Pro: 6 bolts.
21 *Left Flake* 5.7 Pro: Thin to 1.5 inches.
22 *Let it Bleed* 5.10b/c ★ Pro: 5 bolts.
23 *Right Flake* 5.7 ★ Pro: Thin to 1.5 inches.
24 *Mad Dog* 5.10c ★ Pro: 2 bolts.
25 *Cheep Thrills* 5.10a/b ★ Pro: 4 bolts.

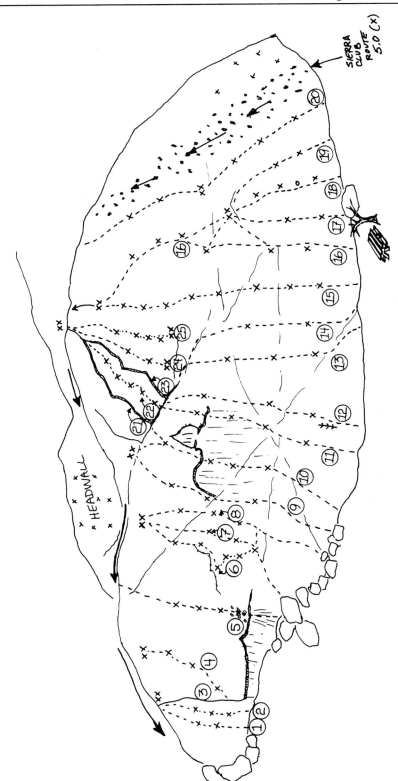

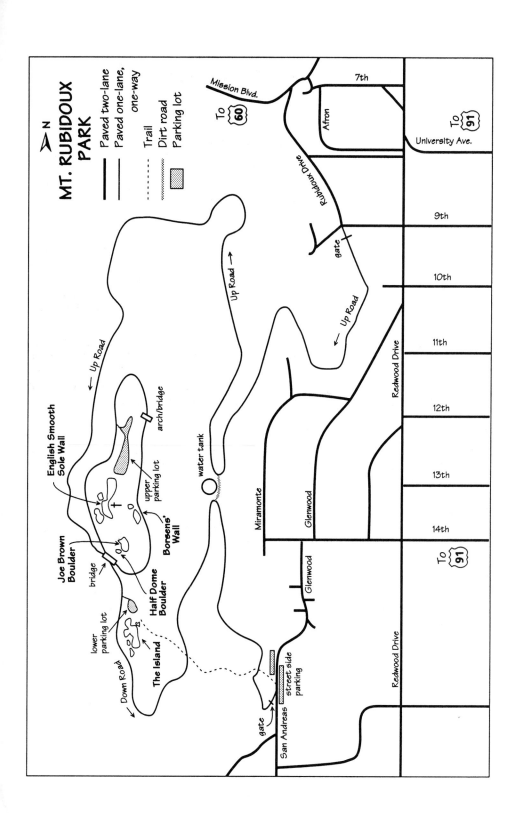

Mount Rubidoux

This popular bouldering area is located in the city of Riverside. Mount Rubidoux is easily distinguished as a large hill with a very large white cross at its top. The hill is strewn with tan-colored granite boulders. There are hundreds of boulder problems up to B2 in difficulty. Most boulder problems are thin face with a few cracks. There are also many top-rope climbs and a few obscure lead climbs.

How to get to Rubidoux

Mt. Rubidoux is easily reached from either the 60 or 91 Freeways near the city of Riverside. See map page viii. A one-way paved road winds its way up and then back down in this city Park. The road is closed on Thursday, Friday and Saturday to vehicles. During the winter, the road is open Sunday 9 am to 5 pm and Monday to Wednesday 9 am to 3 pm. In the summer the road is open on Sundays 9 am to 7 pm. The park is open at all times to foot traffic.

When the road is open, the "up" road is found on Rubidoux Road, best reached from 10th street, just south of University Avenue. Park either at the top of the road (the upper parking lot) or the lower parking area down the hill. If the road is closed, it is best to park along San Andreas street and walk up a rough trail near the down road exit. This trail leads to the lower parking area. See map page 160.

Season

Mount Rubidoux can be quite hot (and smoggy) during the summer months. The best time to climb here is fall through late spring. During the summer, late afternoon bouldering is often pleasant.

Equipment

Shoes and chalkbag. A short rope (100 foot), a few nuts and long slings are useful for setting up many of the top rope problems.

Guidebooks

For more complete information see: *Southern California Boulder Guide* by Craig Fry, which covers Mount Rubidoux and dozens of other bouldering spots in southern California.

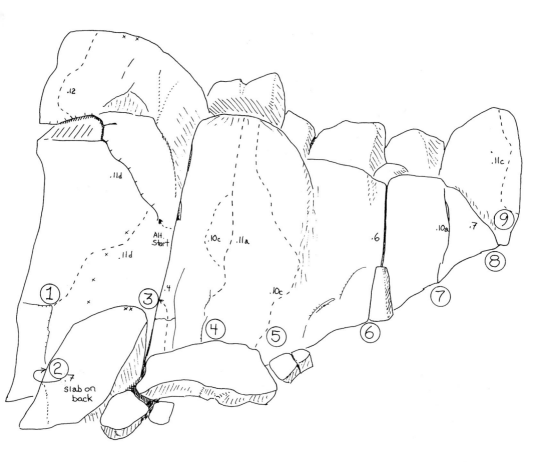

Upper Parking Area
From the upper parking lot, head southwest down some stairs to a trail that heads south among large boulders.

English Smooth Sole Slab
This clean 45-foot slab faces west and is bordered on the left by a wide crack and has several good top-rope face climbs.

1 *A Major Concept* (aka *Cross Rock Traverse*) 5.12a (TR)
2 *Friction Slab* 5.7 (TR)
3 *The Jam Crack* 5.4
4 *Smooth Sole Direct* 5.10+ to 5.11 (TR)
5 *Smooth Sole Right* 5.10+ (TR)
6 *The T Jam* (aka *The T Crack*) 5.6
7 *The Finger Crack* 5.10-
8 *Curving Layback* (aka *Diagonal Crack*) 5.7
9 *Moon* (aka *Skidder*) 5.11+

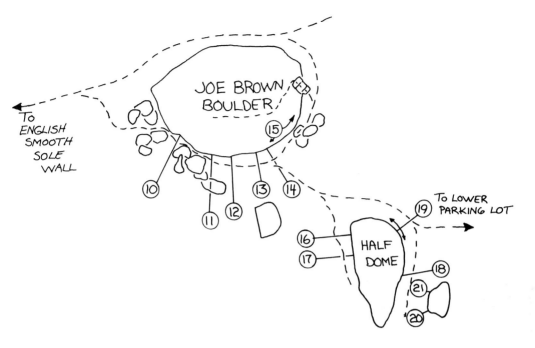

Joe Brown Boulder

This large boulder has several good top-rope problems, and is best reached by heading straight up the step-like stairs toward the cross, then along the ridge for about 60 yards.

  10 *Waterchute* 5.8 (TR)
  11 *Unisloper* 5.11 (TR)
  12 *Cyclops* (aka *The Eye*) 5.11 (TR)
  13 *Power Pack* (aka *The Guanohang*) 5.11+ (TR)
  14 *Face* 5.10
  15 *Face Problems* on the right side (5.6 to 5.7)

Half Dome Boulder

This 30 foot boulder is located 50 feet southwest of Joe Brown Boulder and has two cracks on the steeper north side.

  16 *Left Crack* 5.9
  17 *Right Crack* 5.9
  18 *Trapeze* 5.10 (Cracks/arches on back)
  19 *Various face problems* to right of Trapeze (5.10 to 5.11+)
  20 *Pink Bug* 5.12+
  21 *Black Gnat* 5.11

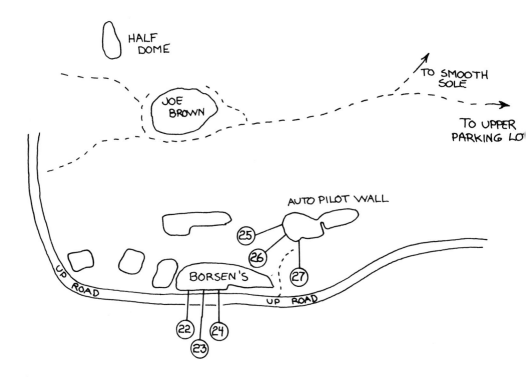

Borsen's Wall Area

Borsen's Wall lies directly next to the "UP" road. The Auto Pilot boulder lies above and right of Borsen's.

Borsen's Wall

22 *Borsen's Left* 5.10
23 *Borsen's Center* 5.11+
24 *Borsen's Right* 5.10+

Auto Pilot Wall

25 *Tail Gunner* 5.12- (TR)
26 *Pilot To Bombardier* 5.11+ (TR)
27 *Auto Pilot* 5.11 (TR)

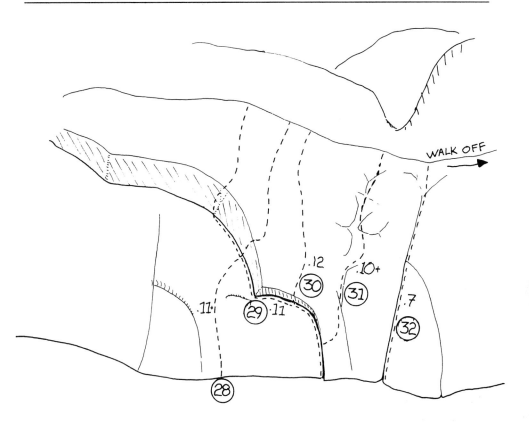

Lower Parking Area

Several good boulder and top-rope problems are found on the complex formation that lies just south of the lower parking area. The best problems are found on the eastern face. If you hike up (on days that the road is closed), the trail takes you directly to this area.

28 **Teflon** 5.11+
29 **Quasimodo** 5.11
30 **Overexposed** 5.12
31 **Kama Sutra** (aka *Five Niner*) 5.10+
32 **The Whoopee Crack** 5.7

The Island Boulder

This 20-foot boulder lies just right *and* slightly downhill from the above problems. The trail from the Lower Parking Lot passes directly under it.

33 **Face Problem** 5.11 Start near the left side of the boulder.
34 **Face Problem** 5.11+ Up the middle on small sloppy holds.
35 **Boulder Seam** 5.9 The weakness near the right side.

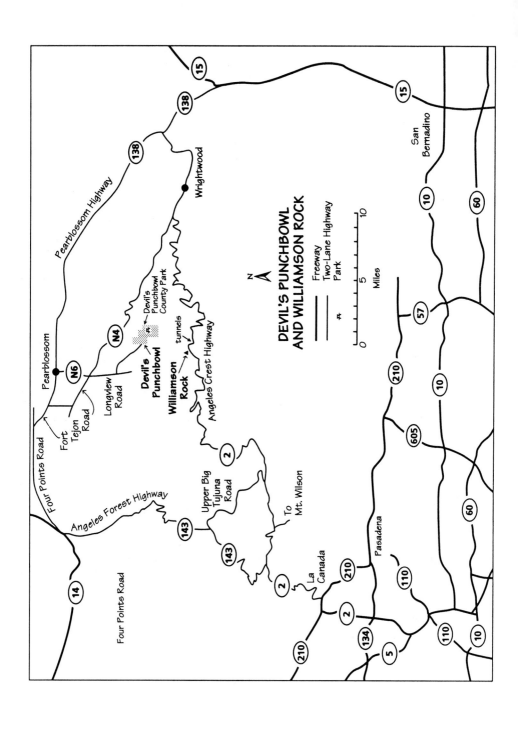

DEVIL'S PUNCHBOWL
AND WILLIAMSON ROCK

N

Freeway
Two-Lane Highway
Park

Miles
0   5   10

Devil's Punchbowl

This area is located in the high desert, near Palmdale and Lancaster, on the northern slopes of the San Gabriel Mountains. Climbing at Devil's Punchbowl sandstone formations has a long history. However, until recently, most climbs were somewhat runout slab routes. In recent years, many fine steep sport routes have been developed on the overhanging faces of the smaller formations in this Los Angeles County Park.

Unfortunately, some local park personnel are strongly opposed to bolting new routes. A moratorium of sorts exists on new route activity pending some long- term solution. Additionally, some of the rock formations lie on private land. Please respect private landowners' privacy. Climbers should refrain from new route activity in the park until some reasonable climbing management plan is formulated by the Park.

How to get to Devil's Punchbowl
From Interstate 14, either head east on Four Points Road to Highway 138 (if coming from LA) or take the Highway 138 exit near Palmdale (if coming from the north). Head south on Fort Tejon Cutoff to reach Fort Tejon Road. Follow Fort Tejon Road east to Longview Road; turn south. Devil's Punchbowl is about 5.4 miles south of here (follow signs). One can also approach Devil's Punchbowl from Interstate 15; take Highway 138 west to Pearblossom, then head south on Longview Road to the park. See map page 166.

Guidebooks
For complete route information see *Guide to Sport Crags in Southern California* by Troy Mayr. For information on older slab routes see *Climber's Guide to Southern California,* by Hellwig and Warstler (not recommended, very out-of-date).

Season
Due to its high desert location, The Punchbowl is primarily a fall through spring climbing area (similar season to that of Joshua Tree). By climbing in the shade, it is possible to climb here most of the year (except on very hot days).

Equipment
Most routes are pure sport climbs; bring appropriate gear.

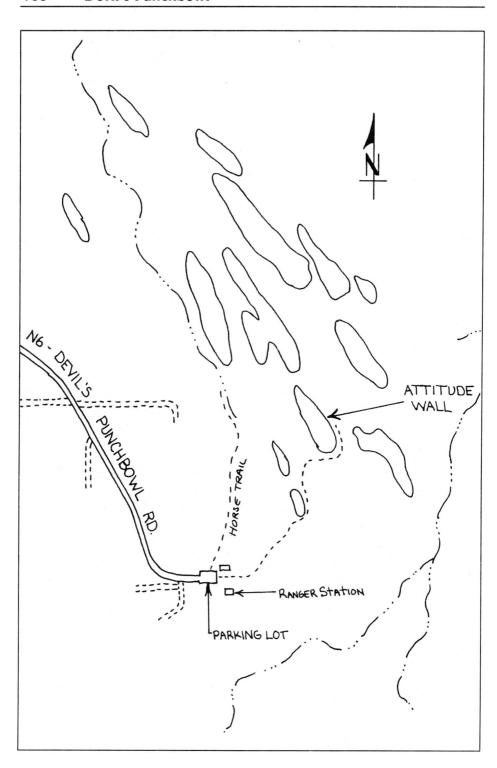

John Mireles

Eric Eriksson climbing at Devil's Punchbowl

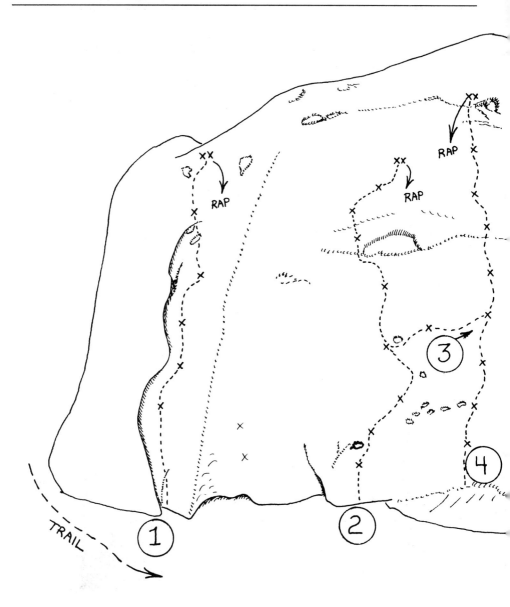

The Attitude Wall

The best routes at Devil's Punchbowl are found on The Attitude Wall, and only these are described. The routes lie on the northeast face of a formation which is north of the parking area at the ranger station. From the parking area head right (around the restrooms), then north over boulders and rough trails to reach the southern part of the rock (See maps page 166 and 168).

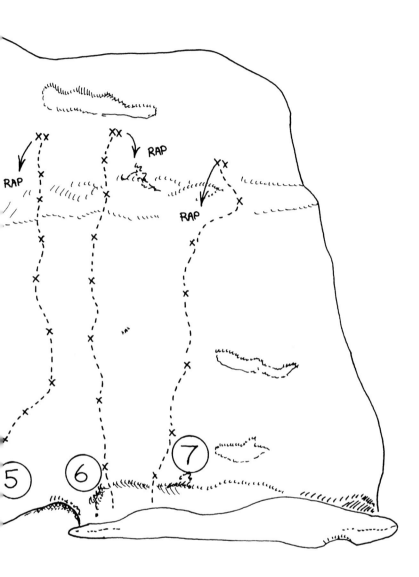

1 *Joke Book* 5.9 Pro: 6 bolts on the left side of the crag.
2 *Best Seller* 5.12a ★★ Pro: 8 bolts.
3 *Best Guided* 5.12d Pro: 10 bolts. Link-up between Best Seller and Misguided.
4 *Misguided* 5.12c ★★ Pro: 8 bolts.
5 *The Attitude Adjuster* 5.12d Pro: 8 bolts.
6 *Stop the Presses* 5.12a ★ Pro: 7 bolts.
7 *Rough Draft* 5.11a Pro: 6 bolts on the right side.

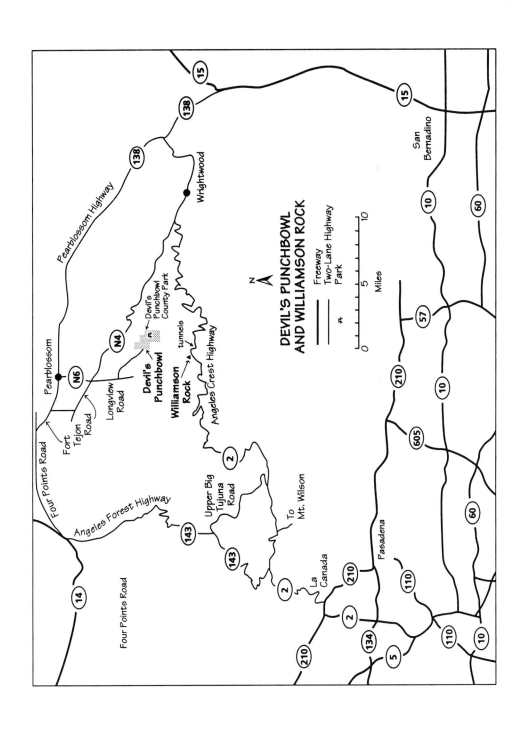

DEVIL'S PUNCHBOWL
AND WILLIAMSON ROCK

N

——— Freeway
—— Two-Lane Highway
✳ Park

0   5   10
        Miles

Williamson Rock

This area is located high in the San Gabriel Mountains a short distance off Angeles Crest Highway (Highway 2). There are over a hundred mostly sport-type routes at Williamson. The rock is somewhat loose, but well-protected. Routes average 70 feet in length, but there are a few multi-pitch climbs. There is a good selection of routes from 5.10 to easy 5.12. The only routes listed here are at the popular London Wall. Route quality is quite variable; the easier to moderately difficult climbs (5.7 to 5.10+) are overall fairly poor in quality.

How to get to Williamson Rock

There are two commonly used ways of driving to Williamson Rock; both involve driving along the Angeles Crest Highway (Highway 2). See map page 172.

From the vicinity of Los Angeles, take the 210 (Pasadena) Freeway to Highway 2 out of La Canada. Drive about 38 miles along this mountain road until you reach a parking area on the north side of the road, approximately 2.2 miles past the Krakta Ridge Ski Area. (From La Canada, it's about 45 minutes to an hour).

From the east, it is much faster to take Pearblossom Highway (Highway 138) off US 15, follow this for 8 miles, then turn west onto Highway 2 (going through Wrightwood) for approximately 25 miles. Just before you get to the parking area, you will go through two short tunnels. (From Wrighwood, it's about 35 to 45 minutes).

From the parking area, a short but steep trail leads along a ridge and down into the streambed below to the base of the rock. Once the ridge and trail become very rough, stay to the right (east) side of the ridge. Do not take the scree slopes directly down to the rock. Stay on the trail! Plan on 5 to 10 minutes to descend to the base. An alternative (not recommended) approach goes down a more gradual trail out of a larger parking lot 0.25 mile farther east along Highway 2.

Season

Due to its location, Williamson Rock is neither climbable nor accessible during most of the winter season. Local conditions will dictate when the road will be open. The best time to visit is in the summer months. A seasonal stream and shady cliffs provide relief from hot days.

Environmental Concerns

Williamson Rock is often quite crowded. Climbers need to organize trail building/defining projects. Please stay on the trail, don't cut down the scree slopes. There are no toilet facilities. Please relieve yourself away from the streambed, and bury all feces. Pack toilet paper out in a resealable plastic bag. Leave the area cleaner than you found it.

Equipment
Most routes are pure sport climbs. Most (but not all) routes end at cold-shut type anchors. With rare exceptions, the only gear required are quickdraws and a 165- to 180-foot rope.

Guidebooks
A complete listing of routes can be found in Troy Mayr's *Sport Crags of Southern California*. If you are other than a very casual visitor, it is highly recommended.

London Wall
From where the trail ends at the stream, head downstream for 75 yards to where the rock lies directly next to the stream. Several good routes are found on this overhanging face which rises directly above the stream.

  1 *Dream Speed* 5.11a ★★ (Beware of rope drag)
  2 *The Final Cut* 5.12b
  3 *Awkward Instant* 5.12a
  4 *Mythic Man* 5.12b ★
  5 *World On Fire* 5.12b ★★ (Stick clip first bolt)
  6 *The Pursuit* 5.12b/c ★
  7 *Liquid Night* 5.12c/d ★★
  8 *Furry Pump* 5.12a ★
  9 *Strange as Angels* 5.11c/d ★
10 *The Labyrinth* 5.11c
11 *KAOS* 5.11b ★
12 *Peace Pipe* 5.10c
13 *Totem Pole* 5.10a ★

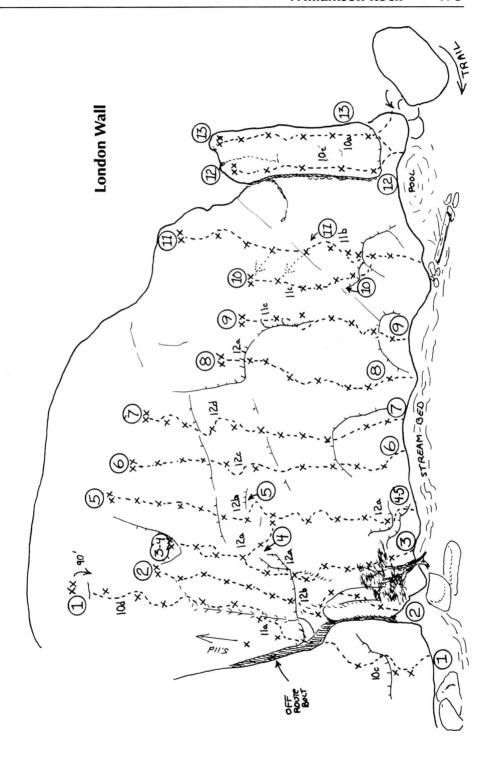

London Wall

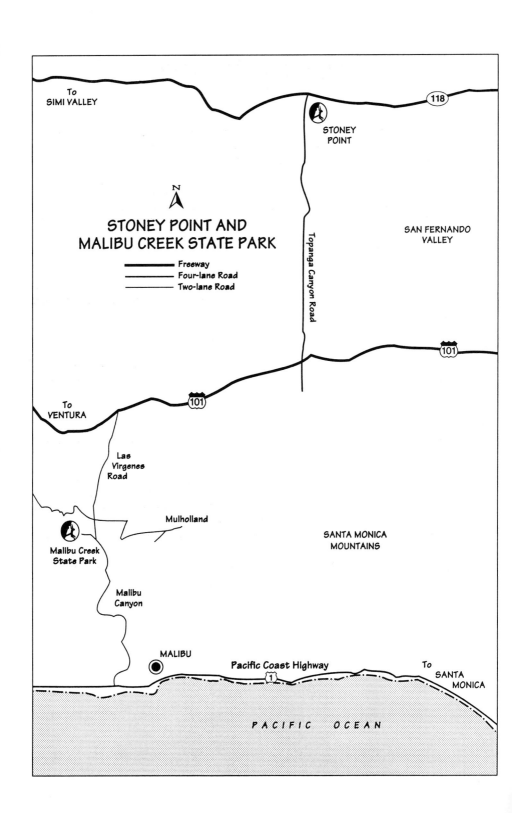

To
SIMI VALLEY

118

STONEY
POINT

N

STONEY POINT AND
MALIBU CREEK STATE PARK

——— Freeway
——— Four-lane Road
——— Two-lane Road

Topanga Canyon Road

SAN FERNANDO
VALLEY

101

To
VENTURA

101

Las
Virgenes
Road

Mulholland

SANTA MONICA
MOUNTAINS

Malibu Creek
State Park

Malibu
Canyon

MALIBU

Pacific Coast Highway

1

To
SANTA
MONICA

PACIFIC   OCEAN

Stoney Point

Climbing at Stoney Point dates back to the 1930's, and was purchased by the City of Los Angles in 1981 as a city park. Many legendary climbers got started on its sandstone boulders: Glen Dawson, Chuck Wilts, Royal Robbins, Yvon Chouinard, Bob Kamps, John Long and John Bachar to name only a few. Stoney remains a popular bouldering and top-roping area for climbers in the Los Angeles area. Literally hundreds of boulder problems and short top-rope routes (up to 50 feet) can be found. Although Stoney Point is undeveloped, it is near a large urban population – so don't expect a garden spot.

How to get to Stoney Point
Stoney Point is located in the northeastern part of the San Fernando Valley on Topanga Canyon Road, just off the Simi Valley Freeway (118). See the map on page 176 for details on how to get to Stoney Point.

Season
It can get extremely warm at Stoney Point during the summer, confining most activity to evening hours or the shady canyons on the north side of the Park. October to May is the best time to visit.

Equipment
Shoes and chalkbag. A short (100 foot) rope, a few nuts and long slings are useful for setting up many of the top rope problems.

Guidebooks
For detailed information, *Southern California Bouldering Guide* by Craig Fry is highly recommended; Stoney Point and several dozen other bouldering areas are covered in considerable detail. *The Stoney Point Guide* (Hellwig and Fisher) is **not** recommended.

A few popular boulders and top-rope problems are listed to get you started. Locals are usually very willing to show you around (and sandbag you).

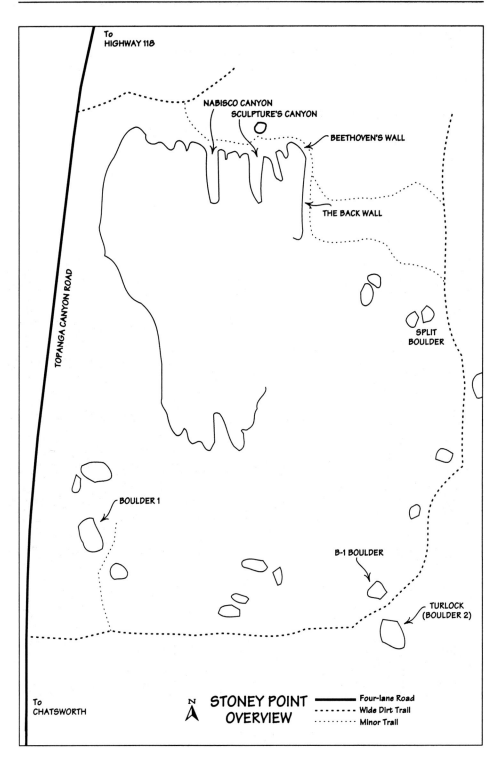

To
HIGHWAY 118

NABISCO CANYON
SCULPTURE'S CANYON

BEETHOVEN'S WALL

THE BACK WALL

TOPANGA CANYON ROAD

SPLIT
BOULDER

BOULDER 1

B-1 BOULDER

TURLOCK
(BOULDER 2)

To
CHATSWORTH

N

STONEY POINT
OVERVIEW

———— Four-lane Road
- - - - Wide Dirt Trail
· · · · · Minor Trail

Boulder 1

This is the large rectangular boulder just below Topanga Canyon Road. Many good problems can be found here (5.5 to 5.11+), as well as a traverse around the entire boulder (5.11+).

Turlock Boulder (Boulder 2)

Numerous excellent boulder problems and a few top-ropes are found on this large boulder, which is located on the southern side of the Park, adjacent to the trail. See map.

B1 Boulder

This lies just a few yards northeast of Turlock Boulder. Good hard problems on the west and south sides. See map.

Ken Powell

Mike Waugh on *Maggie's Farm*

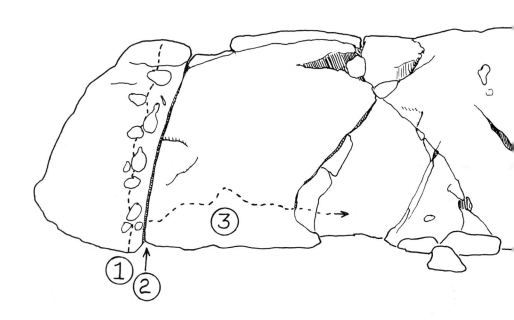

The Back Wall

This long east-facing wall is above the main trail on the east side of the Park. Many good top-rope problems (5.7 to 5.12) and a good traverse on the left side make this a popular spot. See map and topo.

 1 *Pot Holes* 5.9 (TR)
 2 *Pot Hole Crack* 5.10a
 3 *Pot Hole Traverse* 5.10+
 4 *The Plank* 5.12 (TR)
 5 *Vicious* 5.12 (TR)

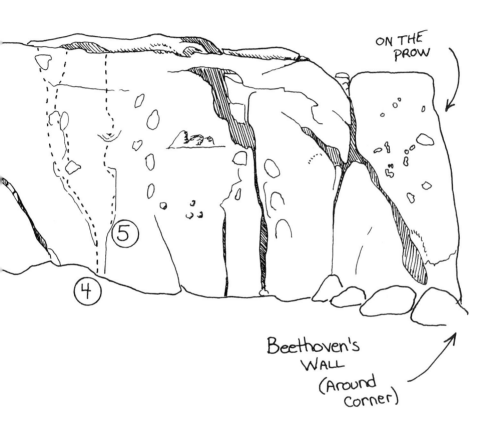

Beethoven's Wall

Just around the corner, facing north.

6 **The Prow** 5.11 (TR) On the extreme left side of the face (on the arête)
7 **Beethoven's Face Center** 5.10- (TR) Up the center of the face.
8 **Beethoven's Face Right** 5.7 (TR) Several variations on the right-hand margin of the face.

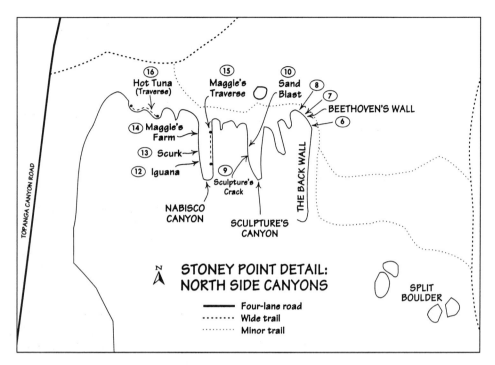

North Side Canyons

On the north side of Stoney Point are several narrow rock corridors. The two largest of these "canyons" (Sculpture's Crack and Nabisco Canyons) have several fine top-rope problems. See map.

Sculpture's Canyon

9   *Sculpture Crack* 5.10+ (TR) This is the left-hand crack on the right (west) side of the canyon.

10 *Sand Blast* 5.11+ (TR) This is the more difficult (and somewhat looser) right-hand crack.

11 *Sculpture Traverse* 5.11- Start below and right of Sand Blast and traverse left beyond the beginning of Sculpture Crack (or vice versa).

Nabisco Canyon

12 *Iguana* 5.11+ Near the left end of the right-hand wall (west side of the canyon) climb solution pockets up and right to a diagonalling crack, then head straight up.

13 *Scurk* 5.12- Climb directly up to join Iguana from the right.

14 *Maggie's Farm* 5.11 On the left end of the wall, climb a wide crack that narrows.

15 *Maggie's Traverse* 5.10+ Located on the left (east) side of the canyon; traverses the entire wall

16 *Hot Tuna Traverse* B1 This excellent traverse lies low to the ground in the deep recess of a low cave. A Stoney Point must do!

Malibu Creek State Park

This excellent climbing and bouldering area is also known as Little Europe, due to the limestone-like pockets on overhanging rock (actually a fine sandstone). The bouldering is very extensive; however, none of the specific bouldering problems are described here.

How to get to Malibu Creek

Malibu Creek State Park is located in the Santa Monica Mountains, between the San Fernando Valley and the coastal town of Malibu, off Las Virgenes Road (also referred to as Malibu Canyon Road). (See map page 176.) The park entrance lies about 2.5 miles south of the Ventura Freeway (101) on your right (west, just past Mulholland Highway). The alternative is to drive north on the Pacific Coast Highway (Highway 1) from Santa Monica past the town of Malibu, then head north approximately 8 miles on Malibu Canyon Road (Las Virgenes Road). If you reach Mulholland Highway, you just missed it.

An entrance fee of approximately $5 per vehicle is charged for entry to the park. Although climbers can save money by parking along Las Virgenes Road, south of the park entrance (0.25 mile extra walk), this is not recommended as car break-ins are common here.

The park is open 8 am to sunset, year-round. However, Malibu Creek State Park can be subject to seasonal fire closures (usually in August to October). For information call either (310) 454-2372 (recorded message) or (818) 706-8809 (park headquarters).

Season

Year-round, although after winter rains the creek may be difficult to negotiate to get to The Ghetto. Park is subject to seasonal fire closures (usually in August to October). Morning or late afternoon are best in the summer.

Equipment

For Planet of the Apes Wall, very long runners (or short rope) and a 150-foot rope. For The Ghetto, quickdraws and a rope.

Guidebooks

For complete information, please refer to Craig Fry's *Southern California Bouldering Guide*. Troy Mayr's *Guide to Sport Crags in Southern California* covers Planet of The Apes and The Ghetto walls (top-roping and leads).

Camping

Camping is available in the park, on a "first come-first served" basis (no reservations). Currently, camping fees are $14 per night.

Planet of the Apes Wall

Named after the movie which was filmed here. See if you can locate many of the remnants of the filming still present in the area. This excellent top-rope wall (no bolts allowed), lies just on your right as you walk on the west side of the creek (cross the bridge by the Visitor Center), about 75 yards south of the bridge. Approximately 10 routes, from 5.11a to 5.12a/b, will be found on the overhanging south face. An excellent boulder traverse along the base (5.11+) is also recommended.

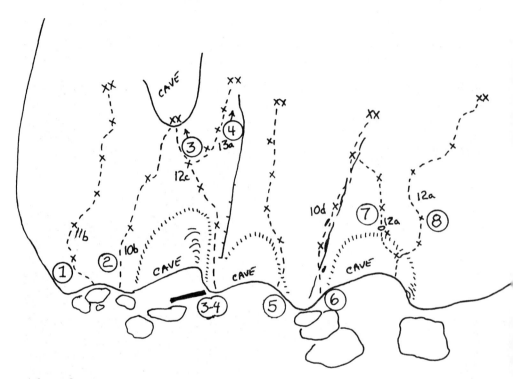

The Ghetto

This fine little sport crag lies farther southwest along the stream from the Planet of the Apes Wall. Just south of the Planet of the Apes Wall is a large pond. An easy fifth-class traverse of the pond's east side or a tricky jump and boulder hop from the west side must be negotiated to reach The Ghetto, some 100 yards downstream of the pond. All routes/variations are not shown.

1 *Skeezer Pleaser* 5.11a/b ★
2 *Kathmandu* 5.10b
3 *Stun Gun* 5.12c/d ★★
4 *Maximum Ghetto* 5.13a ★★
5 *Darkest Hour* 5.12c
6 *Johnny Can't Lead* 5.10d
7 *Hole Patrol* 5.12b ★★
8 *Urban Struggle* 5.12a ★★

Kevin Powell

Bob Williams on 5.11c at Malibu

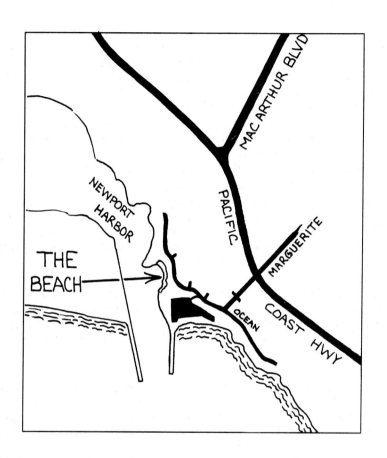

The Beach

Located in the otherwise very sanitized beach town of Corona Del Mar, this area is often littered with the detritus of society. During the summer months it is not uncommon to find used diapers, soft drink cans, and the like all over. Also, this area is just inside the entrance to Newport Bay. As a result, all sorts of interesting things wash up on the otherwise inviting sandy beach.

Because The Beach is often crowded during summer days, climbing is not allowed until after 5 pm or so during the height of the tourist/beach-going season. Please abide by this rule. In this manner, you may avoid falling off that overhang onto someone's beach blanket (or worse, a small infant on a beach blanket).

When conditions are right, the soft sandstone of The Beach provides some of the best bouldering to be found in SoCal. Overhanging problems up to 45 feet high and a sandy beach landing below are the main characteristics. Most problems are in the 10-to-25-foot range, and are almost exclusively done without a rope. A few recent problems have been established with the use of enhanced holds. This practice permanently damages the rock (and established problems) and is strongly discouraged.

The boulder problems tend to be extremely difficult. Still, one quickly learns to master the techniques of balance and strength needed to do even the "easy" problems. Warning: "regulars" at The Beach have the area totally wired. Don't feel too humiliated if the 5.9 problems seem harder than 5.11s you may have led.

Season

Year-round. Climbing at The Beach (also called Pirate's Cove) is a weather-dependent activity. The sedimentary rock tends to soak up moist ocean air like a sponge. On humid or foggy days, the holds will become so greasy that an entire block of chalk may be needed to complete a single boulder problem! The best time to climb is in the afternoon, after dry winds have been blowing. Depending on conditions, one may think that The Beach is either the best or the worst bouldering in California.

How to get to The Beach

Corona Del Mar State Beach is located at the entrance to Newport Harbor. The Beach bouldering area is located in a small "cove" just north of the main beach, inside the jetty. Take Pacific Coast Highway to Marguerite, head west on Marguerite to Ocean Drive. Take Ocean Drive north (right) for several blocks. A large pay parking lot is located below the bluff on the left (west). However, free parking is found along Ocean Drive (north of the entrance to the Parking Area).

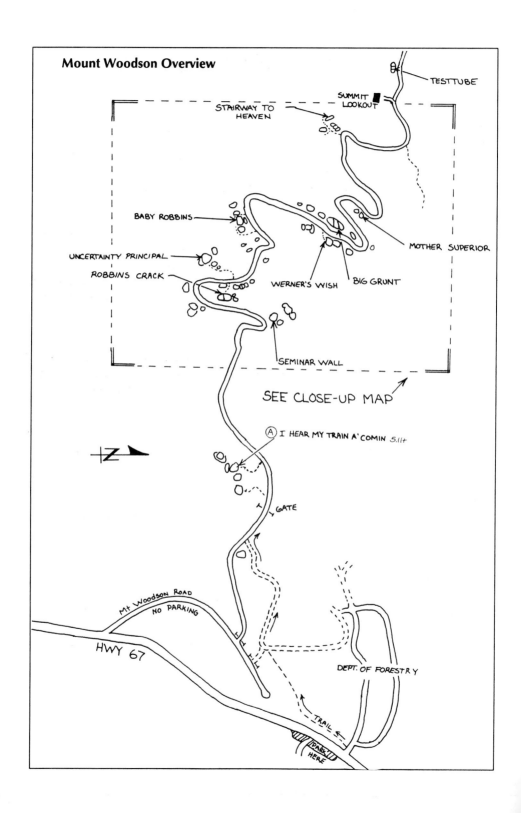

Mount Woodson Overview

TESTTUBE

SUMMIT LOOKOUT

STAIRWAY TO HEAVEN

BABY ROBBINS

MOTHER SUPERIOR

UNCERTAINTY PRINCIPAL

ROBBINS CRACK

WERNER'S WISH

BIG GRUNT

SEMINAR WALL

SEE CLOSE-UP MAP

(A) I HEAR MY TRAIN A' COMIN 5.11+

GATE

Mt WOODSON ROAD

NO PARKING

HWY 67

DEPT. OF FORESTRY

TRAIL

PARK HERE

Mount Woodson

Mount Woodson is much more than a bouldering area, offering a multitude of short top-rope climbs. Although Woodson is best-known for classic cracks, most of the routes and problems are face climbs. The rocks at Woodson are composed of very solid, light tan granite and average 15 to 40 feet in height. Only a few of the hundreds of boulder problems and top-rope routes are described here.

How to get to Mount Woodson
Mount Woodson is located north of San Diego near the town of Poway (see map page viii). Park on the east side of Highway 67, cross the road (watch for traffic) and take a small trail that starts just left of the California Department of Forestry road. Above, a narrow paved road (closed to the public) winds its way to the top of this 3,300-foot hill. The steep road gives access to a myriad of boulders located amidst the brush.

Season
The best time to visit is October to late May when temperatures are cooler. In the summer, temperatures in the 90s and above are not uncommon. Nevertheless, it is possible to find shady areas or climb in the morning or late afternoon even on the hottest days.

Equipment
A short top-rope (100-foot), several very long runners and a little gear for anchors are recommended.

Guidebooks
The best guide to the area is contained in *Southern California Bouldering Guide* by Craig Fry. Keith Bruckner's inexpensive little guide, *Mount Woodson Bouldering*, is also quite good.

I Hear My Train A'Comin Boulder
The following problem is located on a very large boulder above the road amid the vegetation and about 45 yards past the gate. (See map.) A very thin flake on the right is Razor's Edge 5.10d.

    A. *I Hear My Train A'Comin* 5.11+ The overhanging crack left of the thin flake.

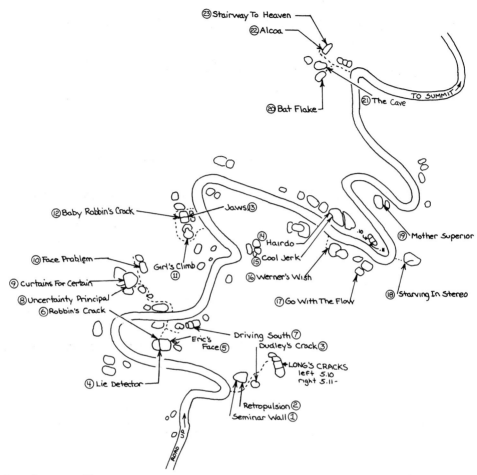

Seminar Wall

This steep boulder with many dark knobs is found to the right of the first sharp left-hand corner in the road.

1 *Seminar Wall* 5.11+ The face problem up the face.
2 *Retropulsion* 5.12 The overhanging arête on the right.
3 *Dudley's Crack* 5.11 Shallow crack lies on the back side of the boulder just right of Seminar Wall.

Robbin's Crack Area

The very large boulder with a crack splitting it.

4 *Lie Detector* 5.12 (5.12 from bottom; upper part 5.10.) The crack on the back (downhill) side of the boulder.
5 *Eric's Face* 5.11- The face problem on the north side of the boulder.
6 *Robbin's Crack* 5.10 The thin hand crack on the uphill side of the boulder (easiest way to the top).
7 *Driving South* 5.11+ The overhanging finger crack below the road.

Uncertainty Principal

This is the huge vertical face that is seen above the road, up and right from the Robbin's Crack Area.

   8 *Uncertainty Principal* 5.11 This is the right-hand of two routes on South Face. Use easy face on east side (1 bolt; one move 5.7) to get to top to set up TR.

   9 *Curtains for Certain* 5.12- Start as per 8, but traverse out left then up.

 10 *Face Problem* 5.11 This lies on the face above and west of the Uncertainty Principal boulder.

Baby Robbin's Area

Take the trail on the left to the boulders hidden in the scrub and oak. Baby Robbin's splits the boulder (Jaws is on the opposite side).

 11 *Girl's Climb* 5.10 On the east side of the boulder east of the Baby Robbin's boulder.

 12 *Baby Robbin's Crack* 5.9 Baby Robbins lies on the South (far) side.

 13 *Jaws* 5.10+ The fingers to thin hand crack on the north side; start in wide chimney-like area.

Big Grunt Boulder

This is the huge boulder with a massive chimney splitting it. Several short face problems can be found on the slab directly below the chimney/boulder, next to the road.

 14 *Hairdo* 5.12 The left-hand of two TR problems on the left-hand end of the east face.

 15 *Cool Jerk* 5.12 The right-hand route.

 16 *Werner's Wish* 5.11- Just before you get to the Big Grunt Boulder, head downhill on the right. Hand traverse right to reach the thin crack above. TR can be set up from atop boulder, reached from road, up a wide crack.

 17 *Go With The Flow* 5.11+ A face problem (TR) on the east side.

Starving in Stereo

Past the Big Grunt Boulder, head straight ahead at the left-hand turn in the road to this boulder.

 18 *Starving in Stereo* 5.12 The diagonal thin crack that peters out.

Mother Superior

 19 *Mother Superior* 5.11+ This overhanging off-width starts down in the chimney-like cavern.

Stairway To Heaven Area

Lies to the left of the right-hand bend in the road.

 20 *Bat Flake* 5.10+ A large curving and detached flake.

 21 *The Cave* 5.11 Up overhanging cave, then up steep face at top.

 22 *Alcoa* 5.11+ The overhanging arête/layback on the right.

 23 *Stairway to Heaven* 5.11+ Up the center of the face on pockets and horizontals.

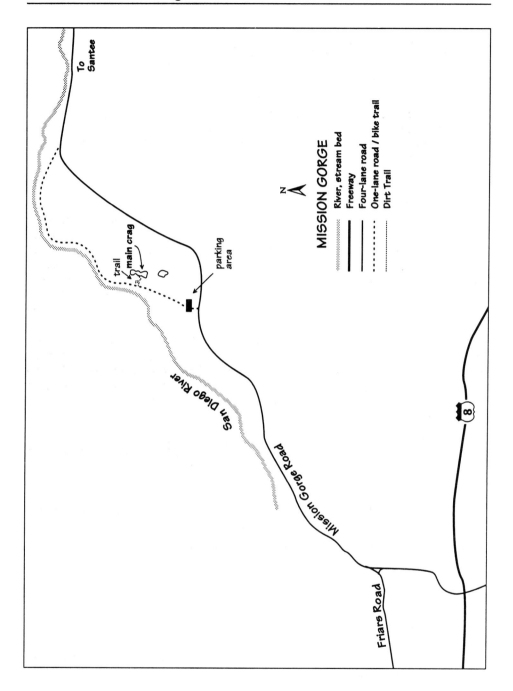

Mission Gorge

This small, west-facing crag lies aside a steep hillside a few miles northeast of the city of San Diego. The Gorge offers lead and top-rope climbs up to 100+ feet high on often slick (but solid) rock. Although there are a few bolted routes (several quite hard), Mission Gorge appeals mostly to local climbers. Most climbs can be (and regularly are) top-roped.

How to get to Mission Gorge

Mission Gorge is located in Mission Gorge Regional Park, just north of Mission Gorge Road. From the 8 Freeway, take the Fairmont/Mission Gorge turnoff and head north. After about 0.75 miles, Mission Gorge Road meets at a "T" intersection with Friars Road. Turn right (this is still Mission Gorge Road), and follow the road for approximately 2.5 miles. The entrance to the park (Father Junipero Serra Trail) and the parking area will be seen on the left (north) side of Mission Gorge Road. Do not leave valuables in your car at the parking area or stay after dusk! Thefts are all too common.

The Father Junipero Serra Trail (a hiking and bike path) is closed to vehicular traffic. From the parking area head north for approximately 0.25 mile. On the hillside to the right (east) are two large conglomerations of rock cliffs. The southernmost cliffs (and the first encountered) are called Middle Earth. The cliff further north is the main Mission Gorge Crag. A steep, switchback trail leads up to the base of the rock.

Bouldering

There is some limited (but good) bouldering to be found near the streambed below the Father Junipero Serra Trail.

Season

The best time to visit is November to April when temperatures are cooler. In the summer, temperatures in the 90s and above are not uncommon, and it can bake in the afternoon sun. Early mornings offer the coolest climbing.

Equipment

A rope, runners and fair selection of gear are recommended.

Guidebooks

Several guides have been done for Mission Gorge. *A Photo Guide to Climbs in Mission Gorge* by David Gerberding is recommended. Bouldering is briefly covered in *Southern California Bouldering Guide* by Craig Fry.

Randy Vogel

Mission Gorge

Santee

This good bouldering area is located just a few miles northeast of the city of San Diego (and Mission Gorge). Santee consists of medium-sized fine-grained granite boulders strewn over a low hillside. Most of the bouldering consists of face and mantle problems. The tallest boulders are about 35 feet high and a top-rope may be useful. It's primarily of interest to locals or if you are already in the area.

How to get to Santee
Take US 8 east to Mission Gorge Road; follow this east (past Mission Gorge) to the town of Santee. Turn left on Mast Boulevard; the boulders are located on the hillside to the north.

Season
The best time to visit is October to late May when temperatures are cooler. In the summer, temperatures in the 90s and above are not uncommon.

Equipment
Shoes and chalkbag. A short top-rope (80-foot), several very long runners and a little gear for anchors can be useful.

Guidebooks
Santee is covered in considerable detail in *Southern California Bouldering Guide* by Craig Fry.

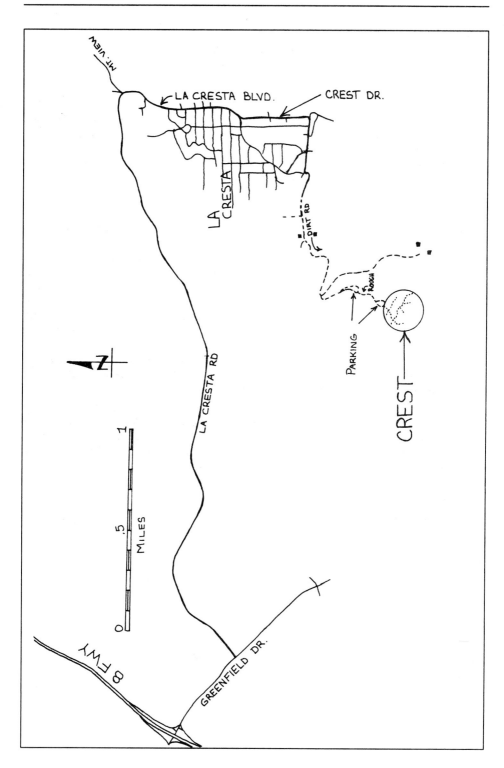

Crest

Once seldom visited, Crest (also known as Singing Hills) has become a popular local area in the last few years. This is primarily due to the increased number of sport-type slab climbs. The rock is good granite, consisting of large boulders and pinnacles up to 75 feet high. Although there are a few excellent crack routes, most of the climbs are either bolted or top-roped face.

How to get to Crest
From San Diego, take US 8 east just past El Cajon to the Greenfield Dr. exit. Head south on Greenfield for approximately 0.5 mile to La Cresta Road; take this east for approximately 3 miles to La Cresta Blvd. Where Mt. View Road intersects, La Cresta Road turns right and becomes La Cresta Blvd.; follow this south for about 0.7 mile. La Cresta Blvd. turns right here; you want to head left (more or less straight), which is Crest Dr. Follow Crest Dr. for about 0.4 mile to where it makes a sharp right-hand turn and becomes South Lane. Head straight (past Albatross) to where the road jogs left, and continue to stay left until the road turns to dirt. Follow the dirt road as it begins downhill and passes some houses. About 0.4 mile past the last houses, the road turns sharply left and downhill; at this point head straight up to a parking area along a ridge. If you have a high clearance/4WD vehicle, you'll want to park as far down the hill as possible, at the lower parking area.

Hike straight up the hillside above parking area to where a trail heads up and slightly right to the "crest" of the hill and just south of a 20-foot-high "finger" of rock (Lone Finger Pinnacle). A trail runs along the top of the hill from here to your left (southeast). The climbs are located on the formations on the hillside below you (on your right – south) as you walk along the ridge. See maps pages viii and 196.

Season
Although it is possible to climb at Crest year-round, most of the climbs face south and can get quite warm during the summer.

Equipment
Quickdraws, very long extension runners, and a small rack up to 2 inches should be sufficient to tackle any of the routes here.

Guidebooks
Crest, San Diego, California, A Climbing Guide to the Singing Hills, by David Goode has a relatively complete listing of routes. Local climbing shops should carry Goode's guide.

Crest

Climbing Gyms
and Artificial Walls

In a very real sense, climbing gyms and artificial walls have become important climbing areas in Southern California. In addition, climbing gyms provide a visiting or traveling climber an opportunity to work out and crank hard even when the weather won't permit. Three southern California climbing gyms are described in the following pages.

Southern California is rife with "glue-on" bouldering and climbing areas, mostly located under concrete bridges. There are upwards of 100 of these areas throughout the southland, most in urban locations. These areas provide excellent training and are quite popular. Unfortunately, several fine areas have been removed by CalTrans (California Department of Transportation). As a result, the locations of artificial areas are left to word of mouth.

Rockreation Sport Climbing Center

Rockreation Sport Climbing Center is one of the largest climbing gyms in the United States, offering over 8,000 square feet of climbing surface and many amenities. It is located just minutes from the 405 and 55 Freeways in Costa Mesa, not far from Orange County Airport and close to bouldering at The Beach in Corona Del Mar. The center has 33 foot-lead and top-rope routes, extensive bouldering and weight equipment. The walls are Radwall design and texture and have a very solid, rock-like feel. A good workout, the friendly environment and full amenities make Rockreation one of the finest gyms in the United States.

How to get to Rockreation
Rockreation is located at 1300 Logan Avenue in Costa Mesa, just off the 405 Freeway. Take the Harbor Boulevard exit from the 405 Freeway and head south to Baker Street. Turn left (east) on Baker, then take a right (south) at College (the first signal). Logan Avenue is the first left (east). Rockreation is located on the left side of Logan Avenue about 0.25 mile from the College and Logan intersection.

Fees
Daily fees are currently $14 per person ($8 for children under 12 years). If you are without shoes, harness, etc., these can be rented. All climbers must take a safety check (free) before being permitted to climb. Other memberships (monthly, semi-annual, yearly, etc.), and student discounts are also available.

Other Features
Men and women's locker rooms, toilets and showers, weight training area, gear rentals, climbing equipment and supplies, cold beverages and snacks. Climbing instruction is also available.

Hours
Monday, Wednesday and Friday
  11 am to 10 pm
Tuesday and Thursday
  6 am to 10 pm
Saturday and Sunday
  10 am to 8 pm
Call for latest hours.
  (714) 556-ROCK

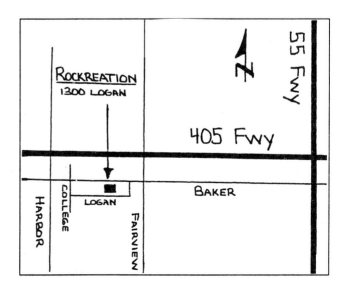

Rock & Roll Climbing Gym

Rock & Roll Climbing Gym in Murrieta was the first real climbing gym to be opened in Southern California, and is the closest gym to popular climbing areas such as Tahquitz, Joshua Tree and Big Rock. You will find lead and top-rope routes up to 24 feet, a lead "roof" and a bouldering cave structure. If you get rained out or desire a change of pace, Rock & Roll Climbing Gym is a good choice. Beginners and advanced climbers will all find a challenge.

How to get to Rock & Roll Climbing Gym
Rock & Roll Climbing Gym is located at 26860 Jefferson Avenue in Murrieta; Telephone: (909) 677-7430, just off the 15 Freeway near Temecula, California. From the north, take the 15 or 215 Freeway south to the Winchester Road exit. Turn right on Winchester Road; Jefferson Avenue is the first right (at the signal).

From the south, take the 15 Freeway north to Winchester Road, turn left (over the freeway), then turn right on Jefferson Avenue (at the signal). The Rock & Roll Climbing Gym is located 0.75 mile down Jefferson Avenue on the right-hand side of the road.

Fees
Daily fees are currently $6 per person. If you are without shoes, harness, etc., these can be rented. All climbers must take a safety check (free) before being permitted to climb. Other memberships (monthly, semi-annual, yearly, etc.) are also available.

Other Features
Changing area, restrooms, gear rentals, climbing equipment and supplies, cold beverages and snacks. Instruction is also available.

Hours
Tuesday and Thursday
    3:30 pm to 10:30 pm
Wednesday
    5 pm to 10:30 pm
Friday
    noon to 10:30 pm
Saturday and Sunday
    11 am to 4 pm
Closed Monday

Call for latest hours.
    (909) 677-7430

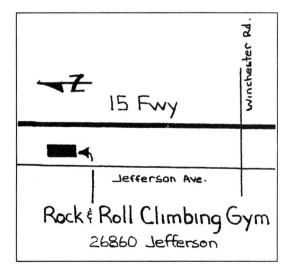

Solid Rock Gym

Solid Rock Gym is one of the best climbing gyms in California and is located just minutes from downtown San Diego, the Zoo and Sea World. It offers 30-foot top-rope routes, bouldering and an incredible lead "cave." The walls have a very solid rock-like feel. An excellent rain-day or evening spot. A good workout and friendly environment can be found for the beginner and advanced climber alike.

How to get to Solid Rock Gym

Solid Rock Gym is located at 2074 Hancock Street, just off the 5 Freeway near Old Town San Diego. From the north, take the 5 Freeway south (just past the 8 Freeway) to the Old Town Avenue exit. At the end of the off ramp, head straight and you are on Hancock Street.

From the south, take the 5 Freeway north to Old Town Avenue exit, at the end of the off ramp head left (over the freeway). Just over the freeway, at the first stop, turn left (south) onto Hancock Street. The Solid Rock Gym is located about 0.2 mile down Hancock St. (through one stop sign), on the left (east). Park along the right-hand side of the street.

Fees

Daily fees are currently $9 per person. If you are without shoes, harness, etc., these can be rented. All climbers must take a safety check (free) before being permitted to climb. Other memberships (monthly, semi-annual, yearly, etc.) are also available. Instruction for all ages and abilities by appointment.

Other Features

Lockers, changing area, restrooms, pay phone, gear rentals, climbing equipment and supplies, cold beverages and snacks. Instruction is available.

Hours

Monday to Wednesday
    5 pm to 10 pm
Thursday and Friday
    5 pm to 11 pm
Saturday
    9 am to 9 pm
Sunday
    noon to 7 pm
Call for latest hours.
    (619) 299-1124

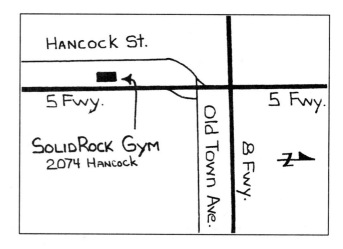

Rated Route Index

5.0–5.5

- B-1 5.1 (Joshua) 62
- B-2 5.3 (Joshua) 62
- Double Crack 5.3 ★ (Joshua) 122
- The Eye 5.3 R ★★ (Joshua) 91
- Fingertip Traverse 5.3 ★ (Tahquitz) 136
- Toe Jam Express 5.3 (Joshua) 122
- Upper Right Ski Track 5.3 (Joshua) 84
- Gotcha Bush 5.4 R/X (Joshua) 122
- The Jam Crack 5.4 (Rubidoux) 162
- Walkway 5.4 R (Joshua) 62
- Angel's Fright 5.5 ★★ (Tahquitz) 136
- Donna T's Route 5.5 (Joshua) 122
- Right On 5.5 ★ (Joshua) 110
- The Trough 5.5 (Big Rock) 158

5.6

- Africa Flake ★ (Big Rock) 158
- Double Decker ★ (Joshua) 70
- Double Dip ★ (Joshua) 99
- Jaws R ★★ (Joshua) 116
- Jensen's Jaunt (Tahquitz) 139
- Linda's Face R (Joshua) 122
- Mike's Books ★ (Joshua) 84
- Puppy Dog (Big Rock) 158
- S.O.B. (Joshua) 122
- Ski Track, Left ★★ (Tahquitz) 139
- SW Corner ★★ (Joshua) 109
- The T Jam aka The T Crack (Rubidoux) 162
- Wedunett (Big Rock) 158
- Who's First R (Joshua) 121

5.7

- Beethoven's Face Right TR (Stoney) 181
- Buissonier ★ (Joshua) 88
- Crater Maker (Big Rock) 158
- Curving Layback aka Diagonal Crack (Rubidoux) 162
- Fingertrip ★★ (Tahquitz) 136
- Friction Slab TR (Rubidoux) 162
- Frosty Cone ★★ (Joshua) 70
- Geronimo ★★ (Joshua) 86
- Hex Marks the Poot aka Lightning Bolt Crack ★★ (Joshua) 104
- Howard's Horror (Joshua) 90
- The Jam Crack ★ (Tahquitz) 136
- Lazy Day ★ (Joshua) 113
- Left Flake (Big Rock) 158
- Mental Physics ★★★ (Joshua) 106
- Mr. Misty Kiss ★★ (Joshua) 70
- Overhang Bypass ★★ (Joshua) 85
- Piton Pooper ★ (Tahquitz) 136
- Right Flake ★ (Big Rock) 158
- Upper Royal's Arch ★ (Tahquitz) 136
- Scrumdillyishus ★ (Joshua) 70
- Steady Breeze X (Joshua) 122
- Stichter Quits ★★ (Joshua) 99
- Tight Shoes R (Joshua) 122
- Tiptoe ★ (Joshua) 62
- Toe Jam ★ (Joshua) 86
- Walk on the Wild Side ★★★ (Joshua) 110
- West Face Overhang ★ (Joshua) 90
- White Lightning ★ (Joshua) 69
- The Whoopee Crack (Rubidoux) 165

5.8

- Baby-Point-Five R/X (Joshua) 62
- Coming Attractions ★ (Owens) 11
- Cranny ★ (Joshua) 62
- Cryptic ★★ (Joshua) 109
- Dogleg ★ (Joshua) 87
- Double Cross ★★ (Joshua) 87
- The Flake ★ (Joshua) 85
- The Flue ★ (Joshua) 91
- Fun Stuff (Joshua) 97
- Hands Off ★ (Joshua) 89
- Leader's Fright R ★ (Joshua) 91
- Mickey Mantle R ★★ (Suicide) 144
- Nurn's Romp ★ (Joshua) 114
- Peyote Crack, Right ★ (Joshua) 94
- R.M.L. ★★ (Joshua) 97
- Rhythm of the Heart X (Joshua) 121
- Right N Up X (Joshua) 122
- Right Sawdust Crack ★ (Joshua) 61
- Sail Away ★★★ (Joshua) 75
- The Sound of One Shoe Tapping (Joshua) 97
- Surprise R (Suicide) 150
- Tombstone aka Pudnurtle (Big Rock) 158
- Traitor Horn ★★★ (Tahquitz) 139
- Up To Heaven R/X (Joshua) 122
- W.A.C. (Joshua) 97
- Waterchute TR (Rubidoux) 163
- White Punks on Dope ★★★ (Needles) 53

5.9

5.12b

- ☐ Bikini Whale ★★ (Joshua) 78
- ☐ Biohazard ★★ (Pine) 29
- ☐ Buffalo Soldier ★ (Joshua) 94
- ☐ The Chameleon R- ★★ (Joshua) 77
- ☐ Conscious Projection (Keller) 155
- ☐ Davy Jones Locker ★★★ (Needles) 44
- ☐ Deity ★ (Pine) 29
- ☐ Dowhatchyalike ★ (Owens) 25
- ☐ Enterprise ★★★ (Owens) 23
- ☐ The Final Cut (Williamson) 174
- ☐ Flashflood ★★★ (Owens) 14
- ☐ Headmaster TR ★★ (Joshua) 109
- ☐ Hole Patrol ★★ (Malibu) 184
- ☐ Mind Meld ★★ (Owens) 23
- ☐ Mythic Man ★ (Williamson) 174
- ☐ Orange Tapestry ★★★ (Keller) 154
- ☐ Particle Accelerator ★★★ (Keller) 155
- ☐ Phasers on Stun ★★★ (Owens) 23
- ☐ Piranha ★★★ (Owens) 21
- ☐ Romantic Warrior ★★★ (Needles) 48
- ☐ Satanic Mechanic ★★★ (Joshua) 81
- ☐ Sea of Tranquility ★★★ (Needles) 48
- ☐ World On Fire ★★ (Williamson) 174

5.12c

- ☐ Apollo TR ★★ (Joshua) 119
- ☐ Baby Apes ★★ (Joshua) 94
- ☐ Caliente ★★ (Suicide) 146
- ☐ The Dark Side ★★ (Needles) 53
- ☐ Darkest Hour (Malibu) 184
- ☐ Dial Africa ★★ (Joshua) 94
- ☐ Dictator of Anarchy ★★★ (Joshua) 118
- ☐ Equinox ★★★ (Joshua) 118
- ☐ Misguided ★★ (Devil's) 171
- ☐ Moonshadow ★★ (Joshua) 114
- ☐ Pieces of Eight ★★ (Needles) 44
- ☐ Piranha ★★★ (Needles) 46
- ☐ The Pirate ★ (Suicide) 147
- ☐ The Pursuit ★ (Williamson) 174
- ☐ Some Like It Hot ★★★ (Joshua) 77
- ☐ The Titanic ★★★ (Needles) 48
- ☐ Warpath ★★★ (Joshua) 65
- ☐ The Watusi ★ (Joshua) 94

5.12d

- ☐ The Attitude Adjuster (Devil's) 171
- ☐ Best Guided (Devil's) 171
- ☐ Eve of the Ring ★★ (Keller) 154
- ☐ Excelsior ★★★ (Owens) 21
- ☐ Father Figure ★★★ (Joshua) 103
- ☐ Headbangers' Ball ★ (Joshua) 109
- ☐ La Cholla ★★ (Joshua) 114
- ☐ Liquid Night ★★ (Williamson) 174
- ☐ Not for Sale aka Borg ★★ (Owens) 23
- ☐ Pink Bug (Rubidoux) 164
- ☐ Pyrotechnics ★★ (Needles) 44
- ☐ Spontaneous Combustion ★★ (Needles) 44
- ☐ Stun Gun (Malibu) 184

5.13a

- ☐ Desert Shield ★★★ (Joshua) 81
- ☐ Ecstasy ★★★ (Pine) 29
- ☐ The Iconoclast ★★★ (Joshua) 110
- ☐ Maximum Ghetto ★★ (Malibu) 184
- ☐ The Moonbeam Crack ★ (Joshua) 94
- ☐ The Powers That Be ★★★ (Joshua) 64
- ☐ Pyromania ★★★ (Needles) 44

5.13b

- ☐ The Avenger (Needles) 44
- ☐ Conquistadors Without Swords ★★ (Owens) 18
- ☐ The Cutting Edge ★ (Joshua) 109
- ☐ Millennium Falcon ★★ (Needles) 53
- ☐ New World Order ★★★ (Joshua) 118
- ☐ Parasite ★★ (Needles) 46
- ☐ Rastafarian (Joshua) 94

5.13c

- ☐ Chain of Addiction ★★★ (Joshua) 64
- ☐ Hydra ★★★ (Joshua) 65
- ☐ Ocean of Doubt ★★★ (Joshua) 64

5.13d

- ☐ G String ★★ (Joshua) 78
- ☐ La Machine ★★★ (Joshua) 64

Route Index